∼ Endo

"Keven's devotional *Brick by Brick* is a 100 space for personal reflection. The devotio...... .... were speaking directly to the post aborted heart. It is beautifully written with a word of encouragement and inspiration for all who regret their decision for abortion."

Linda J. Cochrane, R.N., CEO, author of "Forgiven and Set Free", "Healing a Father's Heart", "The Path to Sexual Healing" and "A Time to Heal".

"I would like to recommend *Brick by Brick Healing His Way Devotional & Journal for Post Abortive Women* by Keven Covert. I love how Keven incorporates hope in every devotional segment. It seems to jump off the page and into the reader's heart. The book is truly a tool that will comfort the sorrow after abortion and also addresses other related problems like sexual abuse and body image. Keven has covered it all, yet she gives a place to reflect and witness your own personal journey – all for God's glory! It is a must have for post-abortive women."

Millie Lace, MSE, LPC
Licensed Professional Counselor
Founder/Director
Concepts of Truth International
Helpline for Abortion Recovery & Prevention

"The heartbreak of abortion runs deep. Keven so sweetly expresses our Father's heart for us as post-abortive women. Her devotions took me right to His heart. Each one touches a place of pain and articulates that pain where I had no words. She has spoken the language of heartbreak, and then the language of healing from the Father's Heart".

Suzanne Howard
National Leader Team
Surrendering the Secret

"When Keven Covert asked me to endorse her devotional, I had no idea how the depth of her words would pierce right to my heart. I am post abortive and have had healing over the years with my participation in several wonderful Bible study groups for post abortive women. As a professional counselor, I am well aware that abortion is a wound to the soul. Since women are born to nurture life, and we choose to end a life, the wound goes very deep. I had the opportunity to use one of her devotionals recently with a post abortive woman who has just begun her healing journey. It brought her to tears and gave her hope that healing is possible. I highly recommend this devotional which is a much needed resource since healing from abortion is an ongoing process."

Jane K. Winn, MSS
Abortion Recovery Director
First Care Women's Clinic, West Palm Beach, Florida

"As a Christian woman who is not post-abortive, I have felt a loss of words that would be meaningful or helpful to a woman who would open up to reveal their wounds over their abortion. I could listen and be a friend who didn't judge their decision, but having no experience in this area, I felt lost. The first devotional I read brought me to tears and helped me to understand a little more of the emotional, as well as the physical pain, a woman goes through during this process. As I progressed through the devotionals, from grieving to healing, the common theme in all of them is love. I recommend *Brick by Brick, Healing His Way* by Keven Covert to any woman, whether you are post-abortive or not. If you are in ministry, this book will help you to understand why it is important to have an open heart to all women who have had an abortion."

- D. M. Smith

"Keven has written on these pages nuggets and truths from her own personal healing journey. This devotional is a tool the Lord will use to heal and restore hearts that have been hurt by abortion."

Cecilia Sullivan
Missionary for LIFE
Certified Abortion Recovery Facilitator

"Brick by Brick is a must have heavenly inspired, spirit lifting devotional which was downloaded directly from the holy Spirit. This devotional brings comfort in so many ways to the spirit and mind that is beyond explanation in words. It gives the peace that one longs to have after years of struggling with the decision of having an abortion and gives the assurance that God is not angry with or at me but rather reveals His grace and mercy. It's truly a reminder that God LOVES me unconditionally."

Monique Strachan Murray - Author of "Soldier of Love Survival Guide", Co-Author of "The Art of Activation", Empowerment Coach & Motivational Speaker

"As you read through each devotion you will have the opportunity to hear from someone who has gone before you on this journey from abortion to healing. Keven's insight and practical helps for healing are invaluable. You will begin to learn God's perspective of you post abortion and how He wants you to heal wholly and completely. Keven has undoubtedly sought the Lord for great insight in writing this devotional. She has captured into words the healing process so that others, such as yourself, may find healing and forgiveness. She helps you to understand healing is a journey and not a destination. As you read, pause to reflect on the words Keven speaks through the heart of the Father, God. Your healing journey begins now! Be encouraged to share your testimony of healing with others."

Reverand Carissa Sangermano
Administrative Assistant to Pastor Candice Manning, Christian Life Center, Ft. Lauderdale, Florida

BRICK BY BRICK

*Healing His Way A Devotional and Journal
for Healing a Woman's Heart*

KEVEN C. COVERT

WESTBOW°
PRESS
A DIVISION OF THOMAS NELSON
& ZONDERVAN

WestBow Press books may be ordered through booksellers or by contacting:

WestBow Press
A Division of Thomas Nelson & Zondervan
1663 Liberty Drive
Bloomington, IN 47403
www.westbowpress.com
1 (866) 928-1240

Scripture taken from the Holy Bible, NEW INTERNATIONAL VERSION® (Life Application Study Bible). Copyright © 1973, 1978, 1984 by Biblica, Inc. All rights reserved worldwide. Used by permission. NEW INTERNATIONAL VERSION® and NIV® are registered trademarks of Biblica, Inc. Use of either trademark for the offering of goods or services requires the prior written consent of Biblica US, Inc.

ISBN: 978-1-4908-6732-8 (sc)
ISBN: 978-1-4908-6733-5 (hc)
ISBN: 978-1-4908-6731-1 (e)

Library of Congress Control Number: 2015901074

Printed in the United States of America.

WestBow Press rev. date: 1/28/2015

Contents

Stormy,

May the Lord use this journey as a road to recovery in many areas of your life. Let the Lord go deep as he holds your hand walking with you. Open your ♡ watch Him heal. The more you surrender—Deeper the healing. Love you Keven ♡

~ Presented to: ~

Stormy Ortiz

From:

Keven Covert

Date:

March 5, 2018

Ezekiel 36:26 This is what the Lord did for me!

Dedication

I dedicate this book to Jesus Christ, my Lord and Savior. It was His vision for this book to be written for the many women who have experienced abortions.

This book is also dedicated to all the women who have the desire to confront their pasts, begin their healing, and go on to claim their victory, which is waiting for them.

⌒ Epigraph ⌒

I will give you a new heart, and put a new spirit in you; I will remove from you your heart of stone and give you a heart of flesh.
—Ezekiel 36:26

You number my wanderings;
Put my tears into Your bottle;
Are they not in Your book?
—Psalm 56:8

The Spirit of the Sovereign Lord is on me,
    because the Lord has anointed me
    to preach good news to the poor.
He has sent me to bind up the brokenhearted,
    to proclaim freedom for the captives
    and release from darkness for the prisoners,
to proclaim the year of the Lord's favor
    and the day of vengeance of our God,
    to comfort all who mourn,
    and provide for those who grieve in Zion-
to bestow on them a crown of beauty
    instead of ashes,
the oil of gladness
    instead of mourning,
and a garment of praise
    instead of a spirit of despair.
They will be called oaks of righteousness,
    a planting of the LORD
    for the display of his splendor.

Isaiah 61:1–3

∽ Acknowledgments ∽

To my godly husband, Kevin; I owe my heart of gratitude to you. As a result of your loving support and encouragement throughout this project, I can say I stayed focused. Thank you for believing in me as we journeyed this road together. Your love and prayers were felt throughout this project. You have sacrificed your time and energy for me, and you rescued me, becoming my patient, personal IT partner for life. I thank the Lord for you daily, my love. You have been that constant in my life; the Lord knew I needed you.

My oldest daughter, Kimberly Covert Corter, you gave me the inspirational idea for the latter part of this devotional. It was the anchor I needed to make this project complete. Thank you for your prayers and support with the call the Lord has given me. Your encouraging talks always came at the right time. The bond we share means the world to me. I treasure your wisdom. You are my beautiful blessing from the Lord.

My daughter Rebecca Covert Wheatley, what would I have done without your endless phone calls and words of wisdom from the Lord? Your timing was impeccable. You journeyed this road with me in a special way. Thank you for your prayers for my healing over the past eight years. You are my faithful prayer warrior and inspirational writer. The Lord used your gift of encouragement mightily during this journey. You are my tenderhearted blessing from the Lord, and my treasure.

My youngest daughter and prayer warrior, Maranatha Covert, you have been with me from the very moment the Lord called me into this area of ministry in February 2012. Your vision continues to inspire me to carry on with the bold calling of this special healing ministry to women. Thank you for your constant intercession and for walking this journey with me. Your words from the Lord were timely. You are my bright, fiery blessing from the Lord; a treasure in many ways. You are the "deal" that was needed from the Lord!

Thank you, Bryan Wheatley, for your love and support throughout this project, and for the times I held your wife captive on the phone. Andrew Corter, thank you for rescuing me this past spring when I thought I was going to lose all the work I had inputted on the computer. I am indebted to you! Thank you for your love and generosity.

Thank you, Jamie Cowhick, for your bright smile of encouragement you have given me since 2012. You saw the passion and always knew something was ahead, believing and encouraging me along my healing journey. You were my first facilitator in this ministry, and now you are a close personal friend, a blessing.

Thank you, Arleen Wong, for being there and believing in me from the very moment the vision for this series came to be. You are an awesome mentor, and I appreciate you. Your friendship means the world as we wait for the Lord to open up doors for us we have yet to explore. Thank you for your prayers, training, and encouragement along this journey. You're a blessing, a special friend, and a sis from our Father.

Thank you, Pastor Tom and Pastor Candice Manning, for believing in me and supporting this special area of women's ministry the Lord has called me to. You have stretched me, and I have grown because of it. I treasure your golden nuggets of wisdom. It is a blessing to be a part of the women's ministry at Christian Life Center and in the areas in which I serve.

Thank you, Cindy Levy, for your excitement and encouraging words over the years, especially the past two, as we began to share together what the Lord was calling me to. I thank you for all your prayers and for believing in me. Thank you, Carlos and Mabel Reyes, for your prayer, support, and guidance in directing me toward the area of ministry the Lord has called me to. Mabel, your constant reminder of "such a time is this" was the words I needed to hear at those moments I saw you. Your smile says it all. Nadine Raphel, your words of wisdom and encouragement mean the world to me. Thank you for your intercession on this journey of healing. Louise Weddington, your listening ear and being led by the Spirit of God are what I needed at those moments during this healing journey. Your reminder of God's timing and that "Mama Louise" hug and word helped me get through those "letting go" moments. Thank you!

Andrea Flores, the Lord knew what He was doing when He had our paths cross—little did we know! Your support in this endeavor from the Lord has been amazing, as He used you to "stretch" me. Your words were always timely and kept me motivated. You have been a constant friend and ministry partner. You're a rare blessing from the Lord. Sharing ministry in various areas with you is exciting and new.

Diana Smith, thank you for your listening ear. Your proofreading brought tears to my heart and comfort to my soul. I treasure your prayers and words of encouragement. Your smile said more than words.

Kemi Onayemi and Monique Strachan-Murray, fellow Christian writers and sisters in the Lord, your words of encouragement and knowledge of what stage I was at in my writing motivated me to not give up; being led by the Spirit when I talked to you kept me going to persevere to the end. Thank you for your prayers of agreement and continued words of love, along with your technical assistance Monique!

I want to thank Gloria Harrington and Charlyne Steinkamp for interceding from the moment this project began. Both of you ladies are full of wisdom and a tremendous blessing. I'm grateful for the prayers you each prayed and your words of support and advice along this journey. You both are treasures of gold, and I have much to learn from both of you.

Thank you, Stephanie Chambers, my new friend from the Lord. Your inspiration helped me at the very end to put the finishing touches on the cover. Your prayers are a blessing from the Lord.

I want to thank Erica Gomez for taking time out from her busy college schedule to write my Forward. Your words of encouragement were more of a blessing than you could ever possibly realize. Thank you for seeing this book from a different perspective. Thank you, *Steven DaSilva,* for creating my heart logo for my ministry and the hours you gave helping me put the finishing touches on this ministry as a whole. You have been a tremendous help and blessing along this journey.

There are many who have prayed me through this endeavor from among my spiritual family at Christian Life Center and my close friends. Thank you. I am blessed to be a part of a spirit-led family of believers.

Forward

During my readings of this book, at first I thought, "I have never been raped nor have I had an abortion! This book does not pertain to me". Oh I was wrong! This book brought healings in other areas of my past that I wasn't aware of!

I am a 25 year old young lady that has never experienced rape, nor have I had an abortion. However, this book brought me to remembrance of other areas of my past that needed to be dealt with. Keven speaks of numbness that comes over our selves when things such as sex, rape or abortion take place. She describes numbness as an emotion we choose to "take over" and in reality it is us not dealing with feeling/pains that clearly need to be dealt with.

During one of the devotions, I literally felt like I was brought back to the place of when I allowed numbness in my life. I remember sitting at the edge of my bed and not feeling a thing... I was 17, and numbed. I knew I was supposed to feel something... But I didn't. The Lord used this book to bring healing! It made me aware and had me remember my past and all for the purpose of bringing my life to another degree of healing, through Christ.

Sex, Abortions and rape are things that happen in women's life that cause shame, hurt to hover over us. If we don't deal with our past with Christ, we are continuing to live in a lie that the enemy has over our lives... Lies that attack our worth, and value! Lies that make us believe that we aren't good enough and that our past has shamed us forever.

Ladies, read this devotional. Let God heal and lead you into a healing or perhaps another degree of healing! God is constantly peeling away layers of our lives, bringing healing. He is constantly tearing away the lies we are believe and restoring us with the truth, His Truth! And all of this is not for "our glory" but to bring healing and restoration to another someone else. Let our lives be a glimpse of His love!! Embark on the process of dealing with the past! Embark on the process of allowing God to bring healings to areas you probably never thought "were a big deal". There is still more, through Christ! This devotional is a phenomenal tool that I believe God has used Keven's life to bring healing and restoration to others!

Erika Melissa Gomez
M.A. Ministerial Leadership
Southeastern University, Lakeland, FL

⟿ Preface ⟿

"I will give you a new heart and put a new spirit in you; I will remove from you your heart of stone and give you a heart of flesh" (Ezekiel 36:26). A new heart I will receive. How is this possible? Besides, with the way my heart started out thirty-six years ago, I was going to need a new heart in order to have any kind of peace and joy in my life. Little was I aware that the decision I made at seventeen would steal my innocence and change my life forever. I had hardened my heart over the years. I could not really enjoy my life the way I should. I needed healing and began searching for the right method.

In 2012, the Lord began to prepare me for my healing from my abortion, which had taken place twenty-seven years earlier. I discovered a Bible Study called *Forgiven and Set Free*, written by Linda Cochrane. It was an intense journey which had me in the Word of God for twelve weeks. My life was radically changed, and my healing from my abortion in 1985 began. I received a new heart of flesh, and the wall that had been built for twenty-seven years began to crumble. As I was going through the study, the Lord gave me a desire to see other women healed. I had a burning passion inside for other women to experience this same freedom I had felt and still feel. I wanted to see women walk in the freedom and go claim the victory waiting for them. Therefore, the vision of this devotional/journal was birthed on July 30, 2013.

As I studied Scriptures in the Bible and sought out the necessary education I needed concerning the various issues associated with postabortion healing and care, the Lord showed me in a detailed vision what my next steps were to be. I participated in two other postabortion Bible studies: *Surrendering the Secret*, by Pat Layton, and *The Journey*, by Millie Lace. I became more determined to begin a journey for other women like me to be set free of their pasts and all the feelings and behaviors that stem from having an abortion. Many women are not aware that some of the behaviors they have now are a result of the experience, which is in their pasts. The feelings of not even acknowledging it ever even took place weigh heavy on a women's heart, and the ugly, shameful secret is never let out or shared with anyone. A wall of denial begins to be built until one day you can no longer carry the burden on your own. It is too cumbersome to bear any longer. Or, it might be the case that deep depression has set in and you cannot seem to swim above water. You feel as though you are drowning in a sea of anguish and guilt. It does not matter which road you have taken, the bottom line is that you need freedom from your pain of all degrees. There is only one way to receive that; it is through the Creator of life, Father God Himself. There is hope and an opportunity to experience unending joy and a peace that surpasses all understanding in your life.

Over the next fourteen weeks, as you read through these pages in the order in which they are written, begin to have a heart of anticipation for your own healing to take place. Be open to all the words which are written. I promise you the journey you are about to embark on in order to take apart the wall you have built up over time, no matter what it consists of, will not be an easy road at times. I suggest you allow that little voice inside to speak to you. The words on these pages are words I received from the Holy Spirit as I spent much time in prayer and reading the Bible while I continued my own journey of healing. After you read the devotion and you find the prayer is blank, share with the Father in your own words what is on your heart and mind. Do not rush this process. Some words you come across will be bold or in italic; when this is the case, it is imperative that you reread the sentence and ponder the true meaning of the thought.

Read the devotions one at a time, and after reading each, begin to pray and reflect on what the devotion spoke to your heart. Use the "Reflection" space to journal your thoughts and insights you gained from the devotion. Begin to embark on this journey toward your healing. Some devotions may speak to you more than others. My prayer is for you to receive the same freedom I have received. Be open to whatever is necessary to take place for your wall to come crashing down over time, healing His way. Claim your victory that is waiting for you. Anything is possible when you put your hope and trust in God. Nothing is too difficult for Him. He is able!

Love and Blessings!

Keven Covert

Part I

The Wall Crumbles One Brick at a Time

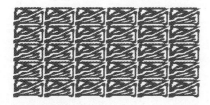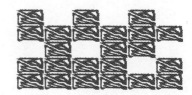

Walk in the Past

I can't bear to recall the devices which took control of me.
As I replay them in my mind, I begin to wonder;
how crazy was I!
Once again, I walk down memory lane of my past.
I can't bear the thought of the screams
and all that took place.
Vivid pictures I see in my mind;
yet most of them are reality.
Emotionless and numb at the time,
feelings being cut off of what was truly happening.

As his little hand reached out
to be touched by my heart, as if to say,
"Let me live, Mommy, I've loved you from the start.
Don't end my life; Jesus has a plan for you and me.
Don't give in to the world's way; it'll work out.
Give me a chance; you will see."

I shut the door,
not listening to that still, small voice.
I've caved in to the unspoken pressure,
and without the Lord, I have no saving grace.
It is the easy way out.
It won't take but a minute in time.
Yet little did I realize all the pain
it would bring to my life.

The wall began to grow thick,
While with each year that passed
the memory of my child sank deeper.
Inside, wondering how long this will last.

I never really let go of him,
though no one ever really knew
the secret that caused me such pain.

Oh Father, help me to walk down my past
and into the pain which lies deep in my being,
all the while knowing You get the glory
and freedom I gain!
Stirring emotions held deep within,
with life coming out from inside.
My heart begins to open up,
no longer hiding behind the pain.
The wall of denial and fear comes crashing upon me;
all along, my Heavenly Father
has His loving arms around me.

Claim Your Victory

The Spirit of the Sovereign Lord is on me, because the Lord has anointed me to preach good news to the poor. He has sent me to bind up the brokenhearted, to proclaim freedom for the captives and release from darkness for the prisoners, to proclaim the year of the Lord's favor and the day of vengeance of our God, to comfort all who mourn, and provide those who grieve in Zion— to bestow on them a crown of beauty instead of ashes, the oil of gladness instead of mourning, and a garment of praise instead of a spirit of despair …

—Isaiah 61:1–3

My daughter, I welcome you with open arms on this journey of healing upon which you are about to embark. It has been a long time waiting, and I knew this day would come. It's time to go back to your past so you can be healed and move forward. Sometimes you have to go back to move forward and go down a road less traveled to claim your victory that is waiting for you. This victory is waiting for many women to claim; you are not alone. One in every three women has experienced the same thing you have or made the same decision. Many areas of your life have been affected by the choice you made or that was made for you. Many women deal with emotional and physiological side effects and concerns from this experience. The guilt and shame you hold deep inside your heart, and the wall of denial you have built around your emotions, will soon be *tumbling down*. The emotional numbness will thaw, and your heart will begin to feel once again.

I know this pain you feel deep inside is too difficult to even imagine touching. Whenever the word *abortion* comes up in conversation, your pain of your past is pushed down deeper into the pit of secrecy. Yet *I will be holding your hand* as you take this journey. My child, I came to set you free from the bondage of your secret. Allow Me to take you down a healing road, a rocky one at that, and I will help you make it smooth. The chains of bondage will be broken, for I came to set the captives free, and it is for freedom that you will gain your victory that is waiting for you.

Prayer: As I begin to walk down this road of healing, I ask that You guide my every step, open up my heart to areas of healing I need, and open my ears so I may hear Your voice in my innermost being. I allow You to stir my emotions locked deep inside so I can begin feel the freedom You talk about. Lead me on this journey of transformation, God, as I begin to heal from my past. I want to heal Your way, God.

 Thought: Which areas of my life will I begin to surrender to God to begin my healing brick by brick?

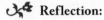 **Reflection:**

The Journey

So do not fear, for I am with you; Do not be dismayed, for I am your God. I will strengthen you and help you; I will uphold you with my righteous right hand.

—Isaiah 41:10

Oh My child, how I long to see you totally healed. It will be a process, a journey you will take while I lead, holding your hand. You will not be alone, for I am with you through all the painful memories that you will encounter. *My love is strong enough for you.* Hold on and get ready for the bumps, scrapes, and bruises. Yet My tender love and mercy will see you through all that is ahead. Depend on Me and My strength, for without Me you are nothing. It is My Spirit in you that will comfort you in times like these.

Nothing is hidden from Me. *I see all.* I see where you've been, where you are now, and where the road of your healing will take you. There is *victory* at the end of the journey. It is My peace, which surpasses all understanding, that will get you through. Let go and let Me be God. Your healing will come in time. The healing process has to begin one stone at a time, one brick at a time, one boulder at a time. Soon the wall of pain will come tumbling down and I will be here to help you build a new heart that is no longer in the dark—a heart filled with light and My love.

Prayer: God, hold my hand and show me how to walk this journey according to Your ways and will for my life. I know You are with me. I need Your loving arms around me as I walk through this journey of healing.

 Thought: What bricks do I need to deal with first? Please show me, Father.

Reflection:

Let Me In

I will give them an undivided heart and put a new spirit in them; I will remove from them their heart of stone and give them a heart of flesh.

—Ezekiel 11:19

It is your heart I love, My dear child. The mere fact that you are willing to read from a broken state tells Me the condition of your heart. Though your heart is rough and *calloused* on the outside, with dark places you have no desire to go to within, I will soften those chambers of your heart and begin to deal with the trauma you experienced. I see your *hardened heart*; I see the deep, dark places of pain you have tried to hide for so long. There is only one thing that can make the pain go away; it is My *forever love and forgiving grace*, which flows from My heart into yours. I took your hardened heart to the cross. It was nailed so I could begin to make it brand-new.

Allow Me to come into the depths of your pain and revisit each situation with you. Surrender to Me the sexual trauma, abuse, addiction, bondages, and insecurities that keep you bound in life. I have the keys to freedom, which the Enemy has tried to keep you from finding; he has kept the chains around your heart for all this time. *The bondage and helplessness you feel will be broken in the name of My Son, Jesus.* He is the one who already rescued you when He yielded His Spirit to Me on the cross for you. He is your *Life Savior.* I am your Savior.

No one comes to My Father except through Me. When you accept My love, I come into your life and *cleanse your heart*, chamber by chamber. Allow My cleansing blood to *enrapture your hardened heart* and begin to make the rough places smooth, the hard places soft, and the stony places fresh with flesh and no longer hard. The stones have built a wall of denial and escape. The denial that has kept you in bondage all these years, not wanting to face the truth, will come slowly crumbling down as you confront the issues at hand.

The time has come to stop running. Run into the Master's arms and allow *My loving embrace* to comfort the hurt and reach inside, giving you a new heart—a heart that can feel and show true emotion. It will be a heart that no longer hides behind the shadows of the past. I will mend your heart so you can learn to love once again and enjoy what I have longed to bless you with.

Prayer: Father, I am ready for a change. I no longer want to be bound to my past. Please begin to work on the walls I have built around my heart. These walls have kept the love I have needed from others away and stopped any more additional pain from penetrating into my being. The only way I can do this is to give You my old heart so You can give me a new one of feeling.

 Thought: Am I truly ready to let go of the old heart of stone and receive a new heart of flesh?

Reflection:

Rest Your Soul

Take my yoke upon you and learn from Me, for I am gentle and humble in heart, and you will find rest for your souls.

—Matthew 11:29

Alone, My daughter? Not a chance; I am right here beside you, holding your heart and wanting to comfort you as the tears flow down your cheeks. Do not stop the tears, for each is *cleansing you* of the hurt that has been covered up for so long. Let the tears flow deep into the crevice of your heart, and watch as My presence softens the memories as you experience them once more. Your healing is beginning from deep within. As the tears begin to *demolish the calloused shell* protecting your heart from painful trauma, you will feel the sting of an anguished past come alive once again. You had buried alive the memories, not wanting to remember that day of long ago. You had buried memories alive, as your worst nightmare ever.

My child, I am here as your *Comforter*, your Father in heaven who knows your every pain and every tear you will shed. I know when you lie down and when you awake. I know your thoughts before you think them. Do not bury the grief-stricken heart any deeper than you have; allow the memories to come bubbling up one at a time, and face them as they are: reality, feelings buried alive, longing to be exposed and healed from within. No longer shove these experiences down deep, never to be exposed and dealt with. Ignoring reality will only cause more affliction and heartache.

Come to Me and give Me your burdens. Accept My gift of mercy and forgiveness. Lay down your shame and guilt, your hate and resentment, at the foot of the cross, along with your deep-rooted anger of rejection. Empty yourself, give them all to Me. I am the shield for the darts the Enemy of your soul discourages you with. When the Enemy comes in like a flood, I will raise a standard against him. I am your *rock and fortress*. Do not be afraid, for *I will be with you along this journey* and show you the way.

I am your identity. I loved you and created you fearfully, and you are wonderfully made. Do not throw away what I created. I do not make mistakes. All I create is perfect. Therefore, My daughter, through My Son, Jesus Christ, you were made perfect in His image. *I am here with you; you are not alone.*

Prayer: Lord, I feel so alone sometimes when I'm in the midst of my pain, as if I'm the only one experiencing this torment. Thank you for reaching out to me and loving me. Thank you for taking on my burdens and beginning to open up the door so I can see the light.

 Thought: What circumstances are surfacing from my memory, from deep within my soul, that I need to lay into the Lord's hands?

🌿 **Reflection:**

Purpose for Pain

The Lord is my rock, my fortress and my deliverer; my God is my rock in whom I take refuge. He is my shield and the horn of my salvation, my stronghold.

—Psalm 18:2

I am with you, daughter, in the midst of the storm. I will not leave you when the situations get tough. I see the tears you shed as it seems as though life is closing in around you and you have no place to turn. Turn to Me, My child; I am here waiting. As the memories come flooding in, seeming to draw you to your past, remember you will not sink, as I am here keeping you afloat on solid ground. For as I hold your hand through the storm, My presence will surround you and *My comfort will be a blanket upon your spirit.* Allow the past to draw closer, one memory at a time. Consent to the beginning of the healing, as it is needed. We will begin with the moment you walked through the door, across the threshold of the clinic, whether you went voluntarily or you were forced and had no choice. It was the beginning of emotional numbness, or maybe the denial had already begun.

Maybe it wasn't denial you experienced, but the reality of what was about to take place—a decision you considered needed to be made and at the same time longed to be over. This decision was made for you, and in your helplessness you believed it to be acceptable. You had no control of what was being done to your own body. In agony you went through the steps of pain. All the while on the outside was a *mask of numbness* you were *hiding behind*; your true emotions of the hurt and depression felt deep within would not surface for a very long time.

I was there with you, though you did not physically see Me. My presence was with your spirit. Remember, I know all your ways and everything about you before it happens. I gave you and others a free will. Though I knew a grave mistake would be made that day and you would feel this way, I did something about it long before the decision was made to end your child's life.

I forgave you, My daughter. I love you still today as much as I did before I created you. *You have a purpose in life,* and I have a plan to give you a future. In this future are hope and My healing touch upon your heart, mind, and soul. I will make you whole. I have set you as a seal upon My heart. *I am your rock and fortress, your deliverer of pain.*

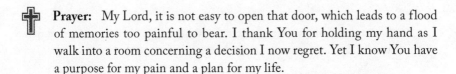

Prayer: My Lord, it is not easy to open that door, which leads to a flood of memories too painful to bear. I thank You for holding my hand as I walk into a room concerning a decision I now regret. Yet I know You have a purpose for my pain and a plan for my life.

Thought: With the Lord holding my hand, which memory am I willing to surrender to Him to begin the healing inside?

Reflection:

"El," Our God

"I am the Alpha and the Omega," says the Lord God, "who is, and who was, and who is to come, the Almighty."

—Revelation 1:8

Who am I? I AM, the great I Am, *Yahweh*. I am a jealous God, and you should have no other gods before Me. *Jehovah Kanna Shemo* has spoken. I am all-knowing. There is nothing I do not see, so call Me *El Roi*. I am always with you no matter what, so call Me *Immanuel*. I have total authority over all the earth; I am the master, the Great Lord, also known as *Adonai*. I am your companion; I am here for those of My creation who love and obey Me; I am *Jehovah-Shammah* to you. I never change, My child, and My promises never fail you. I am *El Emunah*, your faithful God. Put your trust in Me and know Me as *El Elyon* and *Jehovah*, your God who never changes.

When life seems to be coming from all directions and your past begins to emerge from the depths of your heart, call upon *Jehovah-Rohi*, for I am your Shepherd who cares and protects you from the hurt and helps you heal. When despair rises within you and you feel like giving up, call upon *Jehovah-Saboath*. I am *Jehovah-Rapha*, who has already begun to heal you from the depths of your pain. When the wall you have built for all those years begins to crack and fall apart, know that I am *Jehovah-Nissi*, and I will hold a banner of victory for you. Your battles are in the Spirit realm against darkness and light. I will provide you with a peace like no other, an inner peace to your spirit, mind, and soul in harmony. I am *Jehovah-Jireh* and will always be there for you. Call out to Me for help and *Jehovah-Shalom* will answer you and give you the peace you need. Nothing is too difficult for Me, so cry out to your *El Gabor*.

It will get rough in the beginning as you face the situations from the past. Memories will come flooding in, and the Enemy of your soul will discharge you and try to destroy you again. Call upon *Jehovah Tisidkenu*, for you are righteous in My eyes when you believe in My Son, Jesus Christ. You have been set apart, of a royal priesthood, into the family of God. You have been chosen. As you begin to grow in your spirit, rely on Me as *Jehovah Mekaddishkem* as I cleanse you of all your sins. *El Shaddai* will protect you and pour out His blessings upon you. I am the God *Elohim and El Olam*. I am the Beginning and the End, the Alpha and the Omega, the Everlasting God. *I am your Father in heaven.*

Prayer: Father God, as I begin to learn how magnificent You are, I cannot put into words the wonders of Your character and how You touch every area of my life. Your existence is immeasurable, and You amaze me every time I begin to cry out to You. You know exactly what I need and what I do not need. Thank you for always being there and continuing to give me the peace in my spirit I need. Help me to call out to You and remind You of Your promises.

 Thought: Which one of God's many names do I rely on the most and use to call on Father God?

 **Reflection:**

Abba Father

Because you are sons, God sent the Spirit of his Son into our hearts, the Spirit who calls out, *"Abba,* Father." So you are no longer a slave, but a son; and since you are a son, God has made you also an heir.

—Galatians 4:6–7

Who am I? *I am the Almighty God,* the Lord and Creator of the universe and all of humankind. There is none other like Me. I am the *Alpha and Omega,* the beginning to the end. I know all things, I see all things, and I am everywhere at every moment. I am unchangeable and the same yesterday, today, and tomorrow. I am *holy* and without sin. My compassions for you are new every morning. *I am sovereign,* My child, eternal and everlasting. It is through Me that life has its existence. It is through Me you get your power and strength to do as I have ordained you to do. I am in control of all things. Nothing is too difficult for Me. I am *Truth* in action.

I am Love. My relationship with My Son, Jesus, is intimate, and it is through what My Son did for you on the cross that you can have a relationship with Me. Accept My Son's love and forgiveness and I accept you. I created you in My image and want to be intimate with you also. When you see My Son, you see Me. Jesus is your redeemer. I have called you by name.

I know your heart, dear child, and the hidden secrets that live within. My light exposes what you hide in the dark and begins to heal you of all of your pain. I am your *comforter,* your everlasting help in the time of trouble. When the storms of lie come your way, call out to Me and stay anchored to My side. I will protect you and guide you through the waves that try to overtake you. There is nothing I cannot handle. *I am reliable and trustworthy.* Your past is safe with Me. Do not doubt when the Enemy of your soul comes. I go before you and fight your battles as you go through them to claim your victory! I am slow to anger. I discipline because I love you, and the tests you go through strengthen you as you mature to become who I created you to be. I do not show favoritism. I take great delight in you and rejoice when I see the Word fulfilled in your life.

I am your Abba Daddy, your wonderful counselor, and your everlasting Father. There is nothing I will not do to draw you to Me. I am your fortress and protector. I will deliver you from all your fears. Listen to My voice, My child; spend time with Me. I am a perfect God; a good Daddy who loves you with an everlasting love. I will pour My grace onto your life and give you mercy when it is needed. I am your Abba Father; won't you please come to Me? I am here waiting.

 Prayer: God, to learn who you are to me is overwhelming at times. I know you are mighty, yet the more I learn about you, the more I realize Your significance in my life. Continue to pour into me what is fully needed to be able to grasp all You have for me in my life. Begin to teach me Your ways as I walk down this healing journey knowing I am not alone.

 Thought: The God of creation truly is mighty. What can I apply to this healing journey that will prepare me to see each step as necessary to go down along this road I am embarking on?

Reflection:

Pandora's Box

Surely you desire truth in the inner parts; you teach me wisdom in the inmost place.

—Psalm 51:6

My daughter, what areas of life have you put labels on reading "Keep Out" and "Do Not Enter"? Will you open up your heart and allow Me in to see all you need to confront? I already see the hidden, yet I will not force My hand upon you until you are ready. I am a *gentleman* and will be here waiting for you until you are ready to go digging into Pandora's box, as the world calls it, and deal with each issue one at a time. I know how much you can handle. I feel your pain, My child. I see the hurt in your entire being when your mind is flooded with memories from your past. *You no longer have to be locked in the bondage of your past sins. For one element that did not escape Pandora's box was the hope in which I offer.*

Daughter, take *courage* and let Me give you My strength to open up the box, and let us begin to break down together the wall you have been building all this time. The top layer, which is holding down tightly everything layered underneath it, needs to be torn down first. Do you know what that is? Are you ready to get real and truthful with yourself? Are you ready for Me to open up your eyes? You don't want to go there. You don't think I don't know that deep down inside you are ready to close the lid, lock the padlock, and throw away the key, never to be seen again! If you do that, you will be bound to your past forever, never knowing what *true freedom* feels like. You may think you are okay. You may have already even accepted Me as your savior. Yet the truth of the matter is, you need to deal with Pandora's box and allow Me to tear down the wall you have built over all the time since you chose to abort your child. There are issues that stem from your choice that you are bound to and are not even aware of.

My daughter, when you give Me your heart, you give Me everything so I can begin to help you heal and be *set free totally and completely*. Your life may not be how you wanted it to be; you may be dealing with bricks caused by your past. As I begin to change patterns you are accustomed to, awakening old, dirty, or embarrassing moments you've had, ones which have been buried down deep, you will experience uncomfortable situations and try to avoid at all cost having to face the past. I want to *overhaul your heart* and renovate and restore what is inside of you. I want to give you a new heart once and for all. Deal with the pain; do not hide from it. There is hope waiting for you that only I can give.

The only way healing will take place is through spending time with Me. I love you, daughter. You have been forgiven for that which you have locked away. I long for you to make a commitment to Me so I can go with you on this journey. I know you hesitate to open the box; the fear is too much to bear. Again, it is the hope in which I give you that strengthens you on the road to your healing. I care about you. Remember, I know what's inside; it's you who has forgotten.

 Prayer: Lord, as I take one step closer to opening my Pandora's box, please relieve this fear inside of my heart as I reopen my past. I know it will hurt and the pain at times will be unbearable; yet reassure me of Your presence as I walk down this journey of my healing. I want the hope everlasting that is waiting for me once I surrender all over to you.

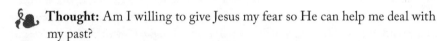 **Thought:** Am I willing to give Jesus my fear so He can help me deal with my past?

Reflection:

Comforting Sorrow

And our hope for you is firm, because we know that just as you share in
our sufferings, so also you share in our comfort.

—2 Corinthians 1:7

I watched as you walked through the door and sat down to wait. I couldn't help
but shed a tear when all along I could feel the fear you held inside. I was right there
beside you, though you did not see Me at the time. I could see the blank stare on
your face, which really said, "I wish I did not have to be in this place." As you sat
there waiting to be counseled, I was talking to you; yet, I was drowned out by the
lies you heard. I could see right through your excuses not to have this child. The
lies the Enemy of your soul instilled in you were alive. I watched as you walked
down the hall; right behind you I stood. I knew in My Spirit that if you could,
you would keep on walking down the hall and not make that turn into the room
of death. I heard you cry and scream of agony from deep inside your being, hoping
the pain you felt would subside. Relief and peace were all you wanted, yet instead
that day you gained nothing but pain and a heartache.

The secret you so longed to keep silent and make go away never really left, and it
has been with you all this time. What you thought would be a quick fix and no
big deal has now become very much a part of you. You handed over your child to
Me, and I was there to receive. I received your baby's spirit and took your little
one home with Me. Although the experience is over, I left you with the memory
of that day.

My daughter let the pain you are now feeling emerge from the depths of your
soul, and allow the tears to flow freely, fully cleansing you of forgotten emotions
that have been buried. Give Me your burdens, your guilt and shame, all those
emotions and circumstances that stem from that day. The day in your past you
tried so easily to shove down in denial has come upon you, revealing the cries of
memories that will arise for healing to take place.

I was with you during the moment you found out you were with child, and *I have
never left you.* I will be here now as you courageously step forward to begin your
healing and to see yourself free of bondage, *living a life of victory.*

Prayer: The pain is too much to bear. Help me, please, to go to the places I have so long wanted to forget. With You holding my hand, Jesus, and giving me the strength, I will depend on You with every step I take.

Thought: What will it feel like in the depths of my soul when I begin my healing to be made whole?

Reflection:

Healing Tears

Those who sow with tears will reap with songs of joy."

—Psalm 126:5

I see your tears begin to gather at the corners of your eyes as you begin to reminisce of memories from your days gone by. Your tears are fresh and warm against your tender cheek. Each one holds a painful memory. Yet somewhere in that tear you shed *a ray of hope*, a promise of a better tomorrow. A tear, when it drops from your face, takes the pain from deep within and removes it from your heart, releasing it into My hand. My hand is big enough to hold all your tears, My dear child. Let them flow; don't stop them from streaming down your rosy red *calloused* cheek. As the tears flood like a river, the very thing that is at the center of your heart, the root of all your emotions, will begin to seep out like sap from a tree. It will begin slowly, anticipating releasing the flood of emotions held captive within. Once the flow starts, it will be hard to contain. ***Let your tears flow. Give each one to Me.***

Your tears are used as *a healing agent* for all the pain of shame locked inside, the embarrassing moments in your life, and the painful choices made in your life. Give Me your tears, and I will turn them into *joy* as you begin to heal from your painful past. It will be worth all you go through and experience as I take you on a journey of healing. *I will not leave your or forget you.* My presence is right in the middle of your emotion. I am ready to help guide you one step at a time, and I will enable you to take many more steps—more than you could possibly imagine.

Prayer: As I begin to dig deep into my heart and show You my pain, please hold my hand and give me the security I need as I walk through this journey of healing. Help me to get in touch with the emotions I have hidden for so long and buried deep within my closed heart. Please begin to make my tears flow once again as healing agents.

 Thought: Am I willing to dig deep enough to remove the root that is the cause of my past pain and choices?

🌿 **Reflection:**

Tears in a Bottle

Record my lament; list my tears on your scroll-are they not in your record?

—Psalm 56:8

I saw your heart when you found out you were with child. It is I who planted the seed there to grow, knowing ultimately what your decision and the outcome of it would be. It was a seed of life for you to nurture and tend to. Though you thought you could not handle this seedling, it was to grow into the image of Me. I knew you before you were born. You were fearfully and wonderfully made, just as your child was. I knew about your child before you were even formed.

I am here to help you deal with your decision not to let the child follow the path of growth. You made the choice to end your child's life. The uncanny thing is, I have been here all along, waiting to receive your pain with *open arms*; to wrap *My loving grace* around you and say "You are forgiven, My child." I forgave you before you even made the decision to end your child's life. I am the Father of unconditional love and am *forever forgiving*.

This was not only your child, but Mine as well. My heart saddens with yours. Cry those tears, My child; let go and I will catch all of your tears and put them into a bottle to save for you. I will write them on the scroll of your heart. Then I will turn those *tears of sorrow* into *tears of joy* one day. I promise, My child, that your healing is not far off. Let Me have that moment when you found out you were carrying My child and you decided to not carry it to term. I want your pain. Through this journey *I will be there every step of the way as you begin to heal.*

✝ **Prayer:** Father, put Your loving arms around me and help me dig deep inside to reconnect with You. I want to give You my pain in exchange for comfort and a journey of healing. Knowing You collect and save each of my tears shows me just how much You care. I know with confidence You will return them back to me one day. Turn my aching heart into healing joy.

🐚 **Thought:** What will my tears, which Jesus will be putting into His bottle for me, consist of?

🌸 **Reflection:**

Your Child I Knew

My frame was not hidden from you when I was made in the secret place, when I was woven together in the depth of the earth.

—Psalm 139:15

My daughter, at birth I ordained your life. I know the beginning to the end. Nothing you have done has surprised Me. I was there, ready to lend a hand, when you discovered there was a little life inside of you. I wanted to comfort you when you needed a Father's hug. My child, I created you and scheduled your days and plans for your life until eternity comes. Just as you were with child, I was the one who gave life to him. I planned your baby's life, or I would not have allowed you to conceive. At the time, you were confused, afraid of the unknown, and unsure of how it would all work out. It wasn't the right timing, according to you, or the circumstances were not good on every front. Yet what no one realized was that it was My timing. I knew what I was doing.

I'm the one who formed your child and knit him together for My purpose. His days were planned and ordained by Me. What you and others thought was a mistake was not a mistake. *I do not create mistakes.* Everything I do is good and perfect in My sight. I had significance for your child's life from the beginning of time. Just as I know your ways, I know your child's ways. Yet I also saw your heart. Deep down inside, it didn't line up with the decision you made. I knew that also. I tell you this not to have you feel shame and guilt, for these things are not from Me but rather from your Enemy. There is no guilt and condemnation from Me; there is only the *life-changing transformation that* happens when you accept My love and forgiveness I have for you.

Acknowledge the life that was inside of you. Begin to break through to the wall of denial that has been developing in your consciousness concerning your child, which was part of your life. Begin to seek Me for answers and allow Me to show you things you do not know. *I am here waiting.* I am Abba Father, all-knowing God, who loves you with an everlasting love.

Prayer: Father, please forgive me for interrupting Your plans for my baby's life. You knew everything I was going to do, yet in all these circumstances you loved me just the same. Surround me with Your comfort and peace, I pray. Please begin to help me get in touch with the false reality that has built up over a period of time. This way I can feel the peace You have waiting for me as I surrender all to You.

 Thought: Since nothing is hidden from my Creator, what is keeping me from sharing all with Him?

Reflection:

I Formed You

For you created my inmost being; you knit me together in my mother's womb. I praise you because I am fearfully and wonderfully made; your works are wonderful, I know that full well. My frame was not hidden from you when I was made in the secret place, when I was woven together in the depths of the earth. Your eyes saw my unformed body; all the days ordained for me were written in your book before one of them came to be.
—Psalm 139:13–16

I love you, My daughter. I truly do. I love you so much I gave you a life long ago. I planned out your life before time began. I even knew when you needed to be born. I have ordained your life with plans to *prosper your future and give you hope*. I will not harm you and will always be by your side, *for I know your comings and goings. I am familiar with all your ways.* There is nothing you cannot hide from Me. I see all your past, and I know where to find you; I even know your future, and I will not harm you.

Are you aware of the truth of how you were formed, or do you believe the lie about a blob of tissue, as do many who were lied to? Were you aware that on day eighteen after conception in your mother's womb was a little tube that began to give you a heartbeat? The very next day, I decided your eyes were to be formed; and on day twenty-one I formed your brain and your nervous system began to perform. On day twenty-six I started to shape your legs and arms. Two days later, I did the same with all your systems. I realized you needed some ears and a little nose, so on day thirty each of them began to grow.

And by day thirty-seven you were almost complete. As early as day forty-two, I could tell if you were a boy. The next day, your brain waves could be recorded.

At week seven I could tell what traits you had received from your mom or dad; your muscles formed and your bones began to grow. Your fingerprints in themselves are unique; no one else has yours at week eight. I knew when you were hungry at week ten, because you swallowed and moved your tongue, making a fist with your palm if caressed. At week twelve you were three inches long. At four months your thumb went into your mouth; you could tell what it tasted like and tell your mom, though she could not hear you. At this time your mother's belly was sore because of all the movement inside. I could tell if you were comfortable by the facial expressions you made when you were dreaming. At five months you were halfway developed; you were twelve inches long and weighed a pound. I could even tell if you had baby-blue eyes and curls of brown hair. You slept and were energetic too. At six months you grew two inches and gained almost another pound. You loved to open and close your eyes, and your teeth began coming in. You were soon up to four pounds and one and a half rulers long.

I formed you, My daughter, as I formed all My creation. You are unique and special, wonderfully made. I made you in My image and loved you from the start. Please accept the victory I have waiting for you so that in eternity we will not be apart.

 Prayer: (Share with the Father of creation what is on your heart.)

 Thought: Am I aware of just how intricate the Creator is when He develops a baby from the moment of conception, even at day eighteen?

Reflection:

Facts or Fiction

...and that they will come to their senses and escape from the trap of the devil, and who has taken them captive to do his will.

—2 Timothy 2:26

My daughter, what were you thinking? Did you have any idea of the consequences of the decision you made? Those involved in your abortion thought everything would be okay and it would all be over in no time. The clinic told you your life could continue like normal, as if nothing ever took place. Do you realize the deception you were in when you walked into the clinic that day? Had anyone ever shared with you what I see from above? I want you to have your eyes opened to the truth of the matter. These statistics are not fiction; they come from collected data.

First, *you are not alone,* My child, because statistics show that one in three women of childbearing age have had an abortion by age forty-five. This is an average of *1.4 million abortions a year,* and this came to be with Roe vs. Wade in 1973. This statistic alone states that over *56 million* babies have died as a result of this choice. This lie stating that the baby is a blob of tissue is not true, for I formed you in your mother's womb and had plans for your child's soul. It doesn't matter what your ethnic background or your spiritual beliefs are. Statistics show that 76% of women having an abortion are of some religious background and belief. Also, 52% of women who have abortions are under 25: 32% are of college age and 20% teenagers.

You may think this alarming, or perhaps it does not catch you at all by surprise. Let us take a look at the aftermath of the Enemy's demise. The clinic had you believe you would never have to worry about this procedure again. If this were true, then why are so many women hurting so? Among women who have had an abortion, 63% walk around in denial, while 73% have experienced depression. I'm sure there are more, because many keep their secret to themselves. Data show that 58% of these women have nightmares, and 62% have had suicidal tendencies. Drug and alcohol abuse is on the rise in this demographic, along with eating disorders. The saddest part, I find, is that 80% of women have self-hatred and *86% walk around in fear that someone will find out their secret.* My creation is walking around in anger and loneliness piled a mile deep. Each year, these statistics continue to grow. These are the results of the Enemy's lie. The deceitful lusts and corrupt principles My children have bought into produce a life of sinful desires, secrecy, and shame.

I sent *My Son, Jesus, to earth to give all humankind a new beginning*. He took upon Himself all your sin and punishment. He died in your place to give you life. You do not have to keep living in any of these lies. Come to Me, and I will give you *loving mercy*, wrap My arms around you, and truthfully tell you, "It'll be okay."

 Prayer: I never realized the truth of what really took place. Thank you for opening my eyes and showing Me all the lies I had believed. Begin to work on me as I travel this journey, knocking down the bricks in my wall one by one until it's flattened to the ground.

 Thought: How mad am I willing to get at the Enemy for all his lies? Am I willing to change so I can walk in freedom one day?

 **Reflection:**

This Season Again

Unless the Lord had given me help, I would soon have dwelt in the silence of death. When I said, "My foot is slipping," your love, O Lord, supported me.

—Psalm 94:17–18

"Oh no, not this again; why does this time of year have to be now? I was just getting better and out of my depression and pain." Do these words sound familiar to you? This time of year is an anniversary for you. Which does it represent to you, death or a birth date? Do you recall the day at the clinic when it all took place? Did unresolved issues come up in the midst of remembering? Does it feel as though your head is pounding like a pressure cooker getting ready to explode, or do you feel an abdominal pain that is hard to describe? Do you find yourself thinking of the child you could have had, and in the midst begin to experience a false pregnancy? How is your relationship with your loved ones? Do you feel the tension rising and your personality changing? Do you find yourself to believe you are alienated from your family although you are truly loved? Emotions begin to arise that have been buried for quite some while. You believed these to be gone until others around you sensed something was wrong.

The denial you feel, which has been covering up all these emotions for years, can be pushed down for only so long before it harms you. You are not consciously aware, My child; these are *subconscious reactions* to your abortion around your anniversary date. You ask, "*Why is each year like this? Shouldn't these feelings be gone by now?*" The answer is simple. You have not had a chance to grieve your loss; therefore, you begin to experience your decision all over again. Do not avoid any longer the fact that you have a child who deserves to be mourned and told good-bye. This is a **brick of healing** that is way up high. As long as it is buried in the *wall of denial*, you won't have to experience it all the time.

Come to Me now, My princess, and allow Me to begin to heal you and remove your anxiety. There is nothing I cannot do for you. Begin to enjoy your life one day at a time. I am here supporting you so you don't fall. I will give you the *joy and peace* your soul has been missing all this time.

Prayer: I do remember these feelings now, always at the same time of the year. Please help me, God, to walk without fear. I want to enjoy my life and all it has to offer. Help me on this journey as I begin to heal Your way.

 Thought: What do I need to do to look at my anniversary date in a more healing way?

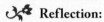 **Reflection:**

Behind the Mask

The Lord does not look at the things man looks at. Man looks at the outward appearance, but the Lord looks at the heart.

—1 Samuel 16:7b

You wear a mask that is as solid as can be. This way no one can look through it to the truth he or she will see. How long do you expect to keep your secret hidden? Do you not realize there is freedom when it is exposed? I know the pain seems endless and it has been in your heart a long time. You think about it constantly, wanting to escape the reality. My child, I have been here all along. I know what you are feeling. It is time to take the opportunity to show your true self, take off the mask of denial, and face your past. Allow the wall to come down brick by brick, dealing with the shame and guilt, and begin your healing. *Give yourself permission to grieve the loss of your child.* It is imperative to set in motion a new beginning. As you begin to uncover what you have been hiding behind, emotions will surface that have been repressed for some time.

It is normal to feel the anger that seems to be emerging. The anger has waited a long time to be let out, waiting to escape. Let go of the feelings of despair, worthlessness, and self-hate. Know that I am here to *give you grace.* No longer do you need to believe the lies of old. I have come to offer you a clean slate and My love for you to behold.

I have forgiven you, My daughter. You were forgiven long ago when I hung on the cross for you to show you My love. I took your place, and the punishment I did receive, to give you forgiveness and everlasting life with Me. Feel the peace I bring to you as you accept My forgiveness for your sins. The grace I give you daily will give you what you need to get you through those difficult places along your healing journey. It is *My mercy I extend to you* that permits you to *be free and claim your victory.*

Prayer: I know it is time to face the truth. It is time to look at my past and begin to peel back the mask I have been hiding behind and let out my secret. I want to accept Your forgiveness and let go. These feelings have defined me for so long that I need to search deep and be set free. Help me, Jesus, as I begin removing each brick one at a time to receive the healing You have for me.

 Thought: What will I see as I remove the mask I so desperately cry out inside to have removed?

 **Reflection:**

Questions Within

Get rid of all bitterness, rage and anger brawling and slander, along with every form of malice.

—Ephesians 4:31

Whom are you angry with? Who told you the forgoing lie that what I created was a blob of tissue and not alive at the time? I am the author of life, and I hold it in the palm of My hands. I knew your unformed body before time began. My daughter, I created you for a purpose, and your child's life also. Although your child is no longer with you, that child is alive, healthy, and happy, spending time with Me in heaven. Your child longs to rejoin with you one day. Do not leave your child motherless. Accept Me as your Creator, your Savior, and your Heavenly Father at most. Experience the love I have for you; do not keep silent within. Express your emotions locked deep inside of you. Get rid of the anger and bitterness, knowing each is safe with Me. You have nothing to hide.

What is under the anger, lying dormant, and at the same time growing in each moment as days pass by? Perhaps you are mad at your parents because it is their fault the decision was made. Maybe if they had found out about the procedure, all the guilt and shame would have been harder to bear. Instead, you hid. Could it be the fear of them knowing and what their reaction would have been? Were you trying to protect your parents' reputation and the betrayal you may have felt? You were not up to being disowned and rejected, so you took the easy way out, or so you thought at the time! You felt you could justify the choice being made with these reasons. This way you could keep on with the goals you had. You had your whole life ahead of you; why ruin it? An abortion would be the easy way out. It would be forever gone and never to be brought up or relived again.

My daughter, whether the choice was yours or someone else's is not what is at stake. The truth of the matter is that the life was not yours to take. Rest at peace and be comforted in your soul. I love you all the same, and nothing can take My love's place. Come to terms with your emotional stress, and I will carry the burden for you. *I will give you a freedom in return that you can't live without. I Am here with you.*

Prayer: Oh, Father in heaven, help me to sort all this anger and fear inside. Show me where it is coming from, and in doing so, I will begin to heal. I am learning to trust You. I need to let out my hidden emotions, which have been hiding for so long.

 Thought: What would it feel like deep in my soul to go about each day with the emotional stress being less than it is now?

Reflection:

Stuffed Passion

"In your anger do not sin": Do not let the sun go down while you are still angry.

—Ephesians 4:26

My daughter, are you mad at Me and won't tell Me so? Do you not know that I am already aware of how you feel? I am the one that created anger as an emotion and gave it freely to you. I am fully aware of the passion it can bring when it rises up inside and you can no longer hide behind it. Yes, there is anger inside of you toward Me. Why would you be mad? Is it because I allowed you to get pregnant? I interrupted your plans, which would cause embarrassment to your family name. If your family members found out, they would disown you—so you thought at the time. They would not be pleased, to say the least, and you could not take the shame. Underlying the anger is the hurt and fear of your parents' condemnation, which you needed to live without. The fear of judgment of others and a scarred reputation was in your foremost thoughts when you came to the reality of the decision you had to make. Are you furious at Me, daughter, for what others did to you when they found out the news? Someone said, *"We need to take care of it."* And you soon realized you had no moment to choose. The choice was made for you, and your baby was forced to be taken from within you.

I see your anger boiling up inside, ready to explode. *Do not let it subside.* Express your emotions and let out the hurt, *no longer stuffing it down*, being stubborn with truth. The truth is, you are mad at Me. It is a powerful emotion I too have used. *Control your anger, and do not sin.* Approach Me, child; I am here, waiting to listen. Give Me your fear, rejection, bitterness, and rage, and I will teach you how to heal from each of them. If you keep hold of these feelings that stem from your abortion, the Enemy of your soul will use them against you.

I still love you, My daughter. I am a Father you can tell your heart to, and I will still love you unconditionally while going through this valley with you. Approach your anger in a healthy manner, giving it to Me, and learn how to *forgive others.* This won't be an easy task, yet I promise this torment and trauma will not last. Jesus loved you so much that He took your trauma to the cross. Be mad, but do not sin. *Open up the chambers to your heart and accept Me in.*

Prayer: How can I be mad at you, God? Yet if it is true, please help me to retrieve all that is inside and give the stubborn emotions to You. It is not easy to admit how I feel right now. Please guide me with Your truth as I open up my heart and share the anger and torment with You.

 Thought: What lies at the core of my heart that I do not want to face? For God says He will give me the grace I need.

Reflection:

Controlled Loving Anger

...And I pray that you, being rooted and established in love, may have power, together with all the saints ,to grasp how wide and long and high and deep is the love of Christ.

—Ephesians 3:17b–18

You ask Me if I am angry with you, if I can love you still, because of the choice that was made. I took My creation and gave you a child to raise, train, love, and behold. Although you now regret the choice that was made, I knew all along, My daughter, this would be the outcome of your baby's life. Though a free will was given to each person involved, I still had hoped for a change of mind and for the end result to be altered. Remember, I am God. I know all things, and nothing surprises Me or catches Me off guard. I know everything about you. I knew the choice the Enemy of your soul wanted to take place—to end your child's life so then you would hide behind a wall of denial, stating the procedure never took place. Or, on the other hand, to live a life filled with depression and regret, wondering how you could ever find comfort and peace. As I said, I knew the choice that would be made, though in My heart I longed for it not to be so. Your free will and the choices made control your destiny. However, it is I who guides you on life's path, instilling in you truth along life's journey.

Am I angry with you? Do I love you still? Of course, My daughter, I love you with *an everlasting love*, with which none can compare. My love for you is as deep as the ocean's floor, as wide as the equator, and never ending. My love is like a waterfall flowing endlessly. My anger is like the rapids that trail down the stream I cut out in the mountain. At times it is as smooth as glass, and at other times it is a raging fury. Am I irritated with you? No, seek Me, your Father, in heaven and read My Holy Word. Seek for the wisdom and comfort that I have for you there. I am ready to lavish and pour into your soul a love like you've never experienced. I will take your pain and use it for My gain. I will use the anger you feel inside to fuel your passion for *My purposes and your benefit*. Let out your passionate fury I give to you. Do not keep it bottled up inside. I am a big God and can handle it all. Do not fear, for I am with you. Do not sin by letting the anger get the best of you, giving the Enemy of your soul control when you do so.

I tell you the truth. *Do not let the sun go down on your wrath.* Bring the intense emotion you have shoved down deep to the surface, and I will crack open the hard, calloused shell that has grown around your heart. Do not allow resentment and bitterness to take root any longer. Remove each from within and hand each over to Me. Do not hold on to them for revenge. Revenge is Mine, My child. Allow Me to begin to heal you from within.

 Prayer: Lord, as I continue my journey to the healing You have waiting for me, please guide my emotions and the passion I'm beginning to feel deep in my soul. Encompass me with Your love as You teach me how to express and handle my anger, this emotion You created and gave to me. Show me how to be angry and not to sin; this is hard, and I do not know where to begin.

 Thought: How can God use my anger for passion and His gain while He continues to lavish His love on me?

Reflection:

Deep Wounded Words Part I

Finally, brothers and sisters, whatever is true, whatever is noble, whatever is right, whatever is pure, whatever is lovely, whatever is admirable- if anything is excellent or praise worthy- think about such things.

—Philippians 4:8

I see your calloused black heart, which holds the abuse that has had you trapped in bondage all these years. I have given you the tools to crack it open and let all the hurt be set free. Within are the words that have been spoken over you, ones that cut to the core of your being—the part that you seem to feel defines you and who you believe yourself to be. These are the words of your past, a life that is *under the blood* and the part *I nailed to the cross*. The words that haunt your spirit and whole being deep inside are nothing but a lie from the Enemy. It is his job to torment you with negative thoughts. I am here to remind you to think on things that are pure and not evil, of good report and not hurting; words that are worthy and edifying, not words that tear down.

You being My daughter, the destruction was caused when you began to receive these words into your spirit and you believed these words to be true in your spirit. The ones you believed to be your true self are the very thoughts I have already begun to heal you from. I came to *heal the broken hearted and to set the captives free*. I've come to you today so that you may begin to be totally set free of the chains of bondage the Enemy has bound you in. Your heart can be set free. Won't you allow Me in and give Me permission to break the chains of bondage and set you free? Reach out to Me; My open arms are outstretched wide, waiting for you to run into them.

Prayer: Father, I can no longer carry around the heavy load these chains represent. Please come deliver me and set me free of my own self-destructive talk.

 Thought: What words from the past need to stay in my past?

 **Reflection:**

Deep Wounded Words Part II

The Spirit of the Sovereign Lord is on me, because the Lord has anointed me to preach good news to the poor. He has sent me to bind up the brokenhearted, to proclaim freedom for the captives and release from darkness for the prisoners.

—Isaiah 61:1

The world says, "Sticks and stones may break my bones, but names will never hurt me." What a lie straight from the Enemy. Bones will heal in the natural way, over a period of time. Over a period of time, the names you were called may be forgotten, yet they will resurface when triggered by the right ingredients. Verbal names and impressions received stay with you and never truly go away, finding themselves resurfacing when the wound is reopened. How much hurt can you handle at one time? *My blood on the cross is the only thing that will heal the hurt and cover your sins as though it never happened.* The memory may never go away, yet you will be healed from the pain. I took its place on the cross.

The blood loosens the chains of the Enemy to set you free. Pain is gone and is replaced with love for the ones who treated you with abusive words and negative impressions and actions, controlling you to believe lies about you. My blood *washes away your past and gives you a fresh start*, a love that covers *all.* Believe Me, My child, freedom is waiting. Repeat those harsh words and give them to Me. Should I repeat them for you? I bring them to the forefront of your memory so you will hand them over to Me rather than shove them deeper into the painful pit of your past. Let go and let Me have them, My child.

I want every word, every ounce of pain, every bit of humiliation you feel, all the unworthiness that is associated with the shame you feel. My love covers it all. Say the abuse out loud. Do not keep the memory locked inside. There is *freedom* when you say it and hear it leave your heart. Say the hurt out loud, hear it leave, and give it all to Me. I receive your pain and give you a fresh thought of who you are in Me.

Prayer: I so desperately want You to take away all the pain I feel inside, Lord. It is so hard to dig deep and go places I've kept hidden for so long. Help me to get in touch with each memory so I can receive the healing You have waiting for me.

 Thought: Where do I need to go digging first in order to unbury the pain so my healing will begin?

Reflection:

Roots of Pain

So if the Son sets you free, you will be free indeed.

—John 8:36

As you lie there in the sunshine, soaking up rays of hope, allow Me to fill your spirit with things from above. I hear your heart cry. It is not very loud at all, but all the while I am listening, My child. I see your heart aching, and I have begun to show you what is needed. *Surrender* all the pain inside; give to Me the memories one by one. The cure you need for your heart will take Me getting inside.

I want to unlock the chains that have you bound to your past hurts and the issues you need to deal with. No more stuffing the abusive words and actions deep inside, a place in which you have hidden all the mistreatment and abuse, which no longer want to reside. Open up your heart and allow Me to come in and begin your healing.

No place is too dirty for Me to be. Once again, let Me in. I will come in and sweep your heart clean from head to toe. What will happen next is for Me to know. Allow Me to tear down the wall you have built one brick at a time with memories that haunt you and won't leave your mind. Please don't change your mind and push Me out, not letting Me in.

I will continue to knock. I am a *persistent* Father. I will *patiently* wait at your heart's door until out of the center comes the root of your pain.

Prayer: Lord, I want to give You the chains that bind my heart shut. I want You to open my heart and let out the pain. Help me get to the root that has caused all this torment I no longer want to have inside. I want to be set free from the part of my past I cannot see because it is buried so deep inside of me.

 Thought: What is at the root of all my pain, and how far down does it really go?

✂ **Reflection:**

Questions of Heart

...to proclaim the year of the Lord's favor and the day of vengeance of our God, to comfort all who mourn, and provide for those who grieve in Zion- to bestow on them a crown of beauty instead of ashes, the oil of gladness instead of mourning, and a garment of praise instead of a spirit of despair.

—Isaiah 61:2–3a

What are you afraid of, child? Is it the silent talk going on you cannot hear? Is it the unspoken words that haunt you daily? Is it not being able to control what others are thinking about you, judging you without ever speaking to you? Is it the continuous rejection you feel from those in your past, or the fact that if they found out what was in your past, you could no longer face them? Do you fear the unspoken shame and guilt you feel to be exposed, and a finger being pointed at you in ridicule, only causing you to feel more humiliated? Do you hide your past pain by pushing it down and covering it up with outside comfort, such as food, alcohol, and promiscuity, only to find after the binge that you feel even worse than before you began? Do you ever find yourself in a state of mind in which you are overwhelmed with the stressors of life and you can't swim to get your head above water, because you are sinking into a pit of depression? Do you have a fear of failure and making mistakes, always longing for perfectionism?

I alone have the answer. Lay down the need *to control* what's going on in your life and *surrende*r these countless *heartrending burdens* to Me. The control struggle is weighing on your heart, preventing your healing. Control has a friend called pride. This pride you carry inside is a coverup for the insecurities you still deal with and try to hide. Yet I see them all. Be secure in Me and allow Me to consume your life and be in control. I know the plans I have for you. Surrender to Me your pride, and I will replace it with humbleness of heart.

Do not become pitiful and hate yourself. Give yourself the opportunity to walk in *beauty and power* and to receive My grace I give to you to go on each day. Walk in the *oil of gladness* and put on the *garments of praise*. Do not believe the lies other speak into your life. I sent My Son to remove all despair from you. *Jesus took it all to the cross.* Put your hope in Him, and allow Me to put on you a crown of beauty and fill your heart with joy!

Prayer: My soul longs to be at peace and filled with this unspeakable joy You speak of. Do whatever is necessary in my life to get me to the place of surrender; to lay these issues of control at the feet of the cross and not take them back. I want to walk in the fullness of life You have made available to me. I surrender my heart to You.

Thought: Is it worth the cost to give up my old ways to walk in surrender to the Lord?

Reflection:

Father Who Knows Our Sorrows

For we do not have a high priest who is unable to sympathize with our weaknesses, but we have one who has been tempted in every way, just as we are – yet was without sin.

—Hebrews 4:15

Are you ready to confront the issues at hand that have you barred? You need to face the fact that you will never be free unless you give them to Me. It won't be easy, My daughter. Together we can tear each level of the wall down one brick at a time. Stop skirting the issues and face the truth once and for all.

Let's deal with the issue of rejection, which is deeply rooted underneath all the other areas of your life; you have kept quiet about it, not wanting to expose it. Who has rejected you and caused all that pain? It is not I, your Lord, for I have been here all this time. Could it be the rejection of your earthly father that you have repressed all these years and not wanted to confront? Did you not feel his love, or was he totally absent from your heart? What did he do to you for all this pain to be there? Daughter, let out the tears. *I see your heart.* I know all things and want you to know that My love and grace are all you need to get you through to the next day. *I will not leave you nor forsake you.* Know that I am here for you always.

Take a moment and ask yourself these questions: Why did you make the choice to give up your child so easily? Would your decision have brought you safety at that time in your life? If you had kept your child, would the shame and guilt outweigh the rejection you would feel? These questions may seem like they are from the painful past. Many times your past predicts your future. I want to help you *change your future* to you a fresh start and new beginning. You need to *heal,* My daughter, and that is what I'm here for. I'm here to walk down these roads with you, taking apart your pain one brick at a time to help you heal. I'm not going anywhere, and *you are not alone.*

There will be others I will place in your path to give you wisdom and a shoulder to cry on. All along, know that they are *My hands extended*, loving you all the same.

Prayer: Father, I hesitate to confront my past because I know it is going to hurt. I want to go down those paths so much, yet at the same time I can feel the wall I have built around me not wanting to move. It causes pain that I've locked away inside. Help me please.

 Thought: What is stopping me from confronting my painful past and not allowing me to be healed?

Reflection:

Deepened Wounds

Here I am! I stand at the door and knock. If anyone hears my voice and opens the door, I will come in and eat with him, and he with me.
—Revelation 3:20

Your wounded heart, My child, I have in My hand. I have been carrying it for you all this time, waiting for you to come forth and give Me all that I have known, which was deep in the depths of your heart. Do not hesitate to give Me your heart. The wounds you have inside need to be brought to the surface and cleaned out. Surrender to Me the wounds concerning rejection and not feeling good enough for the plans I have called you to do, the ones of not feeling worthy enough, so your healing will continue. Give Me the doubt, and let Me heal you of the past. Allow Me to remove all the ugliness and shameful secrets inside each wound and *turn your mourning into dancing and leave your heart overflowing with joy.* Allow My healing touch to rest upon your secrets and heal them with the ointment of My blood, for the blood I shed two thousand years ago is still active and healing today. It is never ending, overflowing in your life.

I love you, My daughter. There are many new things I want to do in your life. Hand over to Me the first hurt you experienced—the hurt that centers around rejection, which is the deepest wound you have. It lies at the bottom of all those wounds on top of it. Some wounds are deeper than others, and I will go as deep as necessary to see that pain come flowing out as My Holy Spirit fills you up and washes you of your past.

Your past can be in My hands, if you allow it to be. Go to those secret places no one sees except for Me. Remember that *I know all about you.* I have My eyes on you, and I see your hurting heart. I'm standing, knocking and waiting for you.

Prayer: Lord, I want You to come open my heart and show me the wounds that need healing first. I know it will be painful, yet I know You are able to relieve me of this feeling of defeat and hopelessness. I want to spend time with You and in Your healing presence. You know all about me and what needs healed the most.

 Thought: What wound would You have me open up first, Lord?

Reflection:

Be Shamed No More

He will wipe every tear from their eyes. There will be no more death'
or mourning or crying or pain, for the old order of things has past away.
—Revelation 21:4

Shame! Shame! Say it louder, My daughter: *shame!* Say it from the rooftops; get
it all out! What caused that guilt? What decision did you make? What are you
running from, and how can I take its place? The truth of the matter is that I
already took its place. *Your shame was nailed to a wooden cross, and the stripes on My
back did the screaming.* No need to feel embarrassed around Me, My princess. I saw
you two thousand years ago as I suffered in your place. Did I have to make the
choice I made? No, yet I loved you enough then to do it anyway because I knew
where you would be today. I knew you would need *My forgiving grace*.

Give to Me openly what I've been waiting to receive. Give to Me all your dirtiness
and shame you no longer can bear. Do not push down the pain deep down inside
any longer, deeper into the pit. This is what the Enemy of the Lord would want
you to do. I love you, My child, and want to keep you from living in torment.
Give Me all of it, and I will release into you My peace and comfort, my solitude
and grace. No more suffering, because I took that all away and took your place.
Come run to Me, tears and all. Allow Me to receive you into My arms. They have
been waiting for you all along.

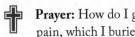

Prayer: How do I give You something that happened so long ago—all my pain, which I buried so deep? Help me to relive the shame and release it to You so I may know this grace You talk about.

Thought: What circumstances are wrapped up in my shame so tightly I won't let it escape?

Reflection:

At the Root

But he said to me, "My grace is Sufficient for you, for my power is made perfect in weakness."

—2 Corinthians 12:9a

I do not want you to dwell on the fact that your parents did not want you and the feelings of rejection that lie inside of you. Though you felt the rejection from your parents, it is I who created you and have plans to use you for *My glory*. The roots of rejection run deep, and out of them grow bitterness and anger. I see the times in your life when you were weak and trying to do everything in your power to be strong. My child, it is not by your power you can do anything; *it is by My power* I give you, and the strength you have from Me when you seek Me, that you become strong.

It is by My spirit inside of you that you are able to do all that I have set out for you to do. Do not hide in your weakness. Give it to Me and *I will equip you with all the tools you need* to dig up bitterness and anger by the root and destroy the Enemy's plans for you once and for all. You no longer need to be kept bound by the past hurts. I have come for you to hand them all over to Me, *your Father in heaven who loves you*. I have come to begin to set you free and allow you to bloom into the woman of God I created you to be.

Prayer: Lord, I need your strength to hand over all my hurts to You. Help me to let go of the past and sense Your strength in my Spirit to do as You want me to do.

 Thought: What lies at the root of my past that I need to turn over to the Lord?

Reflection:

Grace for Pain

Show me the wonder of your great love, you who save by your right hand those who take refuge in you from their foes. Keep me as the apple of your eye; hide me in the shadow of your wings.

—Psalm 17:7–8

I felt your rejection the moment you realized you were having a child. I can still feel your mom's disappointment and hear her question: "Why?" Although you were not a part of your mom and dad's plans at that time, little did they know you were part of My plans.

I have a purpose for all the seeds I plant in a mother's womb. It is always My timing, child, not your parents', for I created you before time began. You were allowed to be born because I have special and specific plans for your life. I needed you to carry out My work and to complete the assignment I have for your life.

I know it has not been an easy road to travel; it has been a journey full of pain and suffering, a road of fear and rejection. I have loved you, child, every step of the way. I have been there with you, holding and comforting you at times you cannot even remember. I soothed your hurts and put a smile on your face. It is through Me that you have received *My amazing grace*—grace to get you through another day. After all the sorrow and tears from the night before, *I encompass you with My joy.*

Prayer: Lord, as feelings of rejection come and flood my being, please show me how to process them and learn to be forgiving.

 Thought: How has the Lord shown me Grace in the midst of my pain?

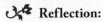 **Reflection:**

Transparency

Blessed is the one whose transgressions are forgiven, whose sins are covered.

—Psalm 32:1

As I begin to tear down the emotional wall that you have built up, I will use it to help you heal from your hurts. Do not fear; let go and allow Me to help you heal from each hurt and every painful moment you have experienced. Know that I am waiting to wrap loving arms around you and replace every pain and emotional scar you carry with a feeling of worthiness and acceptance. My love runs deep inside you, and there is *nothing My love for you cannot heal.*

I remember the first time you gave yourself away, gave your purity away, and you knew deep in your heart it was a mistake; yet, at the time, you would not let the truth surface. I was there. I watched and knew you would have feelings of regret. Loving and forgiving you just the same, I could not make that decision for you. I gave you your free will. I spoke to your Spirit; you would not listen, though I know you heard deep inside. It was that still, small voice reminding you, "I *love you, My child. I am with you always, even now."* It hurt My heart to see you make these choices. Your feelings of wanting to be loved and needed drew you to give of yourself, hoping to feel you were special and accepted, seeking approval in the midst of your sin.

Be *transparent* with Me, My daughter. Do not hide and hold back what you long to get out. The sin you are hiding from is like *poison* in your body. The longer it stays there, the more damage it does. The root of your sin runs deep, and I am here to be the gardener, to remove the cause and help you to grow into the healthy, whole, passionate woman of God I intended you to be.

Remember, I am your Creator, your Heavenly Father. I knew you were weak and would need My help long ago. *It was on the cross that I took your sins to show you how much I loved you.*

Prayer: Lord, help me to remember all the times I reached out for love and was not fulfilled. My heart was still empty and with void. Bring to me stillness in my spirit and lay all my transgressions at Your feet of the cross. In You I have the answers I need. Have Your love consume my spirit and fill the empty void I so long to have filled.

Thought: What am I holding on to that Jesus took to the cross for me and I need to claim my victory for?

Reflection:

The Pain Is in My Hands

My heart and my flesh may fail, but God is the strength of my heart and my portion forever.

—Psalm 73:26

I love you, My child. Do not let go of what I have given you. I am walking this journey with you. There is no way you can do this alone. The subjects are personal; your pain is very deep. The pain is so deep down inside your heart and covered up with lies and escape addictions that I will have to soften the callousness in order to get the cracks to open up. I am here now, stirring up what I need to soften your heart so you will let Me in once again. Do not stay closed and push down your pain that you so long to let out. *Give Me your burdens, My daughter, so I can make your load light.* I love you with an *everlasting love* and am here to comfort you.

As I reveal the past to you, spend time and let the tears flow. You know I catch every tear and put it into your jar. Let the tears of your heart overflow like a river overflowing a riverbank, as if you will drown in the tears. Let yourself be free of past hurts, of all the pain from rejection that is the root of all the strongholds that have tried to cling to you.

I am healing you even now. Hold on tight to Me. I have your heart in the palm of My hand. Let Me help you crack the calloused shell around it so the anguish can come seeping out. The abuse needs to flow out from the inner core to leave you fully pain free. Only I, the Lord, could minister to you this way. You know there is more to come. Let Me have all your memories so I can piece them together in a healthy way and destroy the ones you do not need. *I am your Heavenly Father who knows you better than any.*

✝ **Prayer:** Lord, please help me to release to You the pain I cannot touch deep in my heart. It's hard to face what happened, and I will need Your strength to crack open my calloused heart. Your will, Lord, be done, not in my power but in Yours.

Thought: What is buried so deep I cannot face it?

Reflection:

Eating Your Pain Part I

Ask and it will be given to you; seek and you will find; knock and the door will be opened to you. For everyone who asks receives; the one who seeks finds; and to the one who knocks, the door will be opened.

—Matthew 7:7–8

How would you like a big bowl of chocolate ice cream on top of a chocolate brownie, covered in whipped cream with hot fudge and nuts, and a cherry on top? Then followed by a batch of crunchy cheese nachos with the works? Oh, and do not forget the milkshake and crispy cookies you had from the day before. Sounds like a dessert to Me, daughter; or should I call it like it is—a binge? Do you find yourself grabbing the comfort foods when inside you begin to encounter feelings from the past? The guilt and shame emerge, and the next thing you know, their friends rage, and bitterness appears from out of nowhere. The pain inside is *numbing your feelings to the reality of what you are hiding.* On the outside you are eating the repressed feelings from your abortion, not wanting to deal with them. Once you are done binging and reality comes back into the picture, you purge the unresolved issue and go back into seclusion. Other times, you will keep eating to hide behind the hurt. Then it becomes too late and you end up out of control.

You hate yourself every time you have an episode like this. You feel even more ashamed than before. You are embarrassed by what you did, so the depression gets worse than before. When the guilt sets in, it begins all over again. You never find any real relief, My child; only for a quick fix. *What is eating you inside* is that which is buried and which you are keeping alive. You do not have to keep living like this, in agony and shame. You are dying emotionally. You no longer need to give food power and the control it has on you. When you binge you are not even aware of what is going on. You may just keep eating and never truly understand.

There is hope, My child. Food does not need to be your comfort and way of escape. Substituting the false and quick-fix food binges for comfort, care, and emotional hunger needs to stop. You are harming your physical body as well as your heart. Your body is slowing down and hanging on to every crumb, which draws you to slumber. Food becomes your god, along with your belly.

There is *hope* for this eating style. It is just another brick in the wall that needs to be dealt with. Give Me your time and knock on My door. *Come seek Me* and *you will find Me*; in return I will give you the comfort you need.

 Prayer: God, begin to open up my heart to what is buried alive inside. Reveal to me what I am stuffing and dealing with within my heart. You said there is hope, and I truly want to believe You. It seems that I have tried so many diets, that what is really dying is my insides and emotions. I need healing both physically and emotionally. I know now that You will give me the spiritual nutrition I need to heal my empty heart.

 Thought: Am I ready for a reality check of what has been stuffed inside? What is stopping me so I will not be so blind?

 **Reflection:**

Eating Your Pain Part II

Do you not know that your bodies are temples of the Holy Spirit, who is in you, whom you have received from God? You are not your own; you were bought at a price. Therefore honor God with your bodies.

—1 Corinthians 6:19–20

My daughter, it is time to wake up and take off the rose-colored mask. This mask has been keeping you from growing on the inside and not allowing your body to heal. Are you aware of what you are communicating on the outside to those you have relationships with? You can only hide so long before the truth is found out that you really are not okay and what you really want is help. The tears you cry in private, the tears filled with shame, are ones I see when you feel *trapped*.

Your body is not your own. In fact, when you give your life to Me, I send the Holy Spirit to live inside of you to be your comforter and heal you emotionally. The reasoning behind your eating is simple, and it is time for you to know the answers so you can get your life under control. I know you feel trapped and detest what you are doing; you feel as if there is no hope. Just as when the abortion took place, you felt hopeless just the same.

When you gave away your heart, full of affection, hoping this relationship would last, and then came to find out it had been violated and betrayed, it was no longer full, but empty like a grave. You then found yourself rejected and unworthy and all alone. Food became your *comforter* far within. Food became the only thing you could control in your life. Yet instead of eating to nourish your physical body, it fed your *emotions* instead. Food gave you protection from having to have a relationship, depending on how much you gained. You were safe—or were you?

My daughter, the hidden reason behind why you are eating as you do is that you have not allowed yourself to grieve the way you need to. Grief is waiting to be let out; it is an emotion you need to confront. Purging your body of the food you have eaten, no matter what the method, is unhealthy and will not alleviate the problem. Allow your body to grieve the loss instead of pushing your child's loss away.

My Son came to die for you and take the pain of your abortion to the cross. You will be forgiven, yet healing still needs to the place. There are issues in your life that are a result of the experience you had. Do not run from them; allow Me to help you heal instead. Your body is My temple, and I will begin to heal you one emotion at a time. Rely on Me and trust Me; *I will not fail you,* My child.

 Prayer: I need help, and I cannot do this on my own. I realize now that I am hiding behind my food and not facing the truth. I desire down deep to take care of my body. Please continue to pull out of me on this journey what I do not need. If my body is Your temple, Your guidance is what I need. Show me how to grieve in a healthy manner so I can begin to honor You with my body, both physically and emotionally.

 Thought: Where do I need to go that has held me captive for so long emotionally? Am I willing to let go of false comfort to grow in areas healthily?

✿ **Reflection:**

In My Form Part I

But the Lord said to Samuel, "Do not consider his appearance or his height, for I have rejected him. The Lord does not look at the things people look at. People look at the outward appearance, but the Lord looks at the heart."

—1 Samuel 16:7

Your body belongs to Me. I made you in My image. I do not create unworthy rubbish. I designed every facet of your body to be a certain way. It is not tainted, unattractive, or tattered. You are My beautiful creation. Your beauty was created from within; it came not only from your outer appearance. "Beauty is only skin deep" is a lie. *Your beauty, My daughter, is inside your soul,* the heart of who I created you to be. Do not believe as the world tells you. Do not get caught up in your image and what others see in your outward appearance. Rather, focus on what I have created in you on the inside. Look to Me to see how you are to look. Besides, beauty is in the eye of the beholder, as many have said.

I behold your beauty every time I look at you and see your heart. I see beauty that you cannot see at the moment. One day soon in time, you will see what I see. As your healing takes place, more truth will come to light. Then what I long for you to see will be apparent. The scales will be taken off, and you will see reality in front of you, which is what I see now. You are My masterpiece, My beautiful princess, the apple of My eye.

Prayer: Lord, help me to see myself the way You see me. I give to You the lies others have spoken over my life and ask You to set me free so I can become the woman of God You created for me to be.

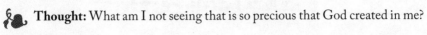 **Thought:** What am I not seeing that is so precious that God created in me?

Reflection:

In My Form Part II

But he said to me, "My grace is sufficient for you, for my power is made perfect in weakness." Therefore I will boast all the more gladly about my weaknesses, so that Christ's power may rest on me.

—2 Corinthians 12:9

I see you walk by the mirror and think the thoughts you do, wondering if you are living up to the standards others have put on you. Now that you are grown, you are the woman of God I created. Let go of the insecurities of what you look like physically and give them to Me. I will *lighten your burdens* and your fear of not being accepted and beautiful enough. I have created inside of you a beauty that compares to no other. It is your physical appearance you want to change, isn't it? If you, My child, will do exactly as I have asked and give Me the negative impressions placed upon you by close family members and friends, by society and what it calls beauty, and if you give Me your fear of never being able to get a grip on your emotional eating and running to food for comfort, I will set in you a new thought process dealing with how to handle emotionally what is set before you. I will give to you a new freedom of emotional healing and the correct mind set.

I am releasing in you a *healing* like none other, a deliverance that comes only from the Holy Spirit. My Spirit has the power to *set you free* from your past memories and your present discomfort with yourself. These effects are still present because you are still holding on to the things that are no longer needed in your life. When you are set free, you will feel lightness because I have the burdens and you will see a change begin to take place. Do not keep taking back the burdens. Lay them down at My feet once and for all. I will not force you. I am a gentleman and am waiting on you, My daughter. Through My strength you will be able to surrender all to Me that is weighing you down. You will see a change in your appearance and mental thoughts. With My help and strength, all things are possible in My power alone. Hold My hand, and we will do this together.

Prayer: Lord, once again I cry out to You and ask for help with this pain I feel. I long inside to be who You have created me to be, to believe with my whole heart and being, knowing that with You all things are possible. Father, place inside my mind your thoughts toward me and Your power in my will. I want to experience this peaceful healing that You have waiting for me.

Thought: How deep into my past is far enough to go in order for my healing to begin with my image of me?

Reflection:

Mindful Image

I delight greatly in the LORD; my soul rejoices in my God. For he has clothed me with garments of salvation and arrayed me in a robe of his righteousness, as a bridegroom adorns his head like a priest, and as a bride adorns herself with her jewels.

—Isaiah 61:10

Do not be shameful of the body I gave you, for it is from Me. I created you in My image, My daughter, and all things I create are *good and perfect* in My sight. Do not let what happened to you when you were younger determine who I have created you to be today. You are lovely, beautifully and wonderfully made. You are My bride, whom I am preparing for my return. Like Esther was prepared for the King, so shall I prepare you for the rest of your time here on earth until I return for you. Your beauty is in the eye of the beholder. The men in your past have abused your body both emotionally and physically. I am here to *heal your wounds and mend your brokenness.* I will clothe you with My righteousness. I am the one who will show you how to be clothed spiritually and who will guide you physically.

Do not be ashamed of your past and the thoughts that haunt you. Do not any longer allow those images of days gone by to resound in your mind. These images are not from the Lord your God. I will remove them as far as the East is from the West. I am the Father who will clothe you in purity and holiness. I will help you take captive the thoughts the Enemy has used against you. I will cleanse your mind and begin to purify your thoughts. *The battle is in your mind.* Your Enemy wants to keep you bound to your past; this is why you need to surrender all to Me. *When you are weak and need help, I am strong.* I long for you to seek My Word and learn how to live a holy and righteous life in Me and Me alone. All things are made new when you become My daughter.

Prayer: Lord, take my corrupted thoughts of my body image and purify them. Begin to plant seeds of Your image for me in my thoughts, and have me grow as a pure woman of God.

 Thought: Am I ready to surrender the old, comfortable me, allow God to purify me, and take on the image of Christ?

Reflection:

Heavenly Relief

No one who hopes in you will ever be put to shame.

—Psalm 25:3a

"It is over. It is gone. No more confusion. I can get on with my life and find meaning again. The burden is gone, and I have relief. Everything is going to be all right." How long, My child, did this comfort last? Did the loss of your child bring you a reprieve in your life? Yet you were only to discover that this procedure you went through would forever be with you. At the time, someone wanted to alleviate the problem; only you found out later that that relief would last only for *a fleeting moment in time.* Then reality set in and the pain of your loss was too much to bear. You tried to forget what you had done, though you had nowhere to run.

You picked up the bottle hoping to *drown your pain away,* only to find in the morning that nothing had changed and a headache remained. You needed that next fix, and most of the time you weren't sure where you would get it from next. You ran to the kitchen for the next bite of *comfort,* only to feel worse than you did before. You searched high and low, from hookup to hookup, never really finding the love you were in need of. You wanted so much for the relief to come back and not to have to face this pain.

Daughter, the pain you now feel is the guilt and shame of what took place. You have tried to cry it all out; however, it seems to always stay. You feel remorse, and your emotions are in turmoil. Turn them all over to Me, and I will begin to *set you free.* Do not build up the wall of denial any longer. Let us together begin to tear down what is there. No longer will you have to run to an unfulfilled escape. I will give you the grace, My child, to get through each difficulty and help you embrace reality when the past exposes its ugly face. I promise you that as you hand over to Me each brick of suffering in your wall of denial, I will replace your *tears of sorrow and mourning with tears of joy and blessing.*

I love you, My daughter, with an everlasting love—a love that comes only from your Heavenly Father up above. I am your *Comforter, your Everlasting Peace.* Give Me your burdens, and I will give you rest and grace to make it through the days with strength and peace.

Prayer: Oh, Father, I do want to believe You are the one whom I can run to. I know I need to totally trust You. I want Your grace to get me through and finally let me be at peace. Begin to tear down the wall of denial and relieve me of my depression. There is no quick fix to help me to heal, and I realize that now. You are the only one who can give me the comfort I need and fix me with Your forgiving grace and mercy when I least deserve it. Please show me how I can receive.

 Thought: As the wall of denial begins to come down, what will I then do to hold on to the Father's love to get me through?

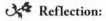 **Reflection:**

Defective Choices of Love

> Put to death, therefore, whatever belongs to your earthly nature: sexual immorality, impurity, lust, evil desires and greed, which is idolatry.
> —Colossians 3:5

Your heart is empty and needs love. Something is missing, and up until now you did not care where the missing piece came from. You desire the affection and security it brings, yet so far you have not received these things. All you have left after all this time is one heart broken into two. Inside your heart, My daughter, are the pure desires of fun, freedom, and emotional trust you want to share with another. The problem in the past was that when you began to open up, you were taken advantage of and the relationship turned into lust and immoral behaviors. Your heart was so desperate for emotional contentment that you gave into impure temptation, and so the cycle began.

The cycle of unclean thoughts led to intentions, and instead of abstaining, you engaged in sinful behavior. This behavior had consequences that you pushed away from the forefront of your mind. All you cared about was keeping your flesh without pain. It was a vicious cycle you were caught in. The Enemy of your soul works hard at getting you to fall. Giving in to temptation may be fun, though it is devastating for all those involved. Sexual promiscuity is just one of the sins you found yourself in. This was not your first thought when all this lustful behavior began.

All you wanted to obtain was *emotional security*, but it was never there, because of the choices you made; you found love in the wrong places. Your heart was harmed in many ways, and your personality changed. You got to a point where you did not care. You lived two lives; you put on the mask and showed only one side.

I know you, My daughter, and I see the ache your heart holds. As much as you have tried to have the perfect relationship, it never seems to be the right one. Your heart no longer engages with emotion; you have no feeling and no pleasure when sexual relations are involved. Your decisions become unwise, and sexual desire is lost for the man you have chosen. The act of coming together with one you care about becomes a ritual, and eventually you become sexually broken, never truly fulfilled. Yet do you not know your body is your husband's to treat with respect?

My daughter, there is only one way to become sexually fulfilled. You need to come to Me and repent and give Me all your defilement. There is hope for your future, and it is in the palm of My hand. Put your trust in Me, and *I will restore what was stolen from you.*

 Prayer: Oh God, help me to give You all the abuse and hurt I have been exposed to. My heart is heavy, yet there are times I feel so detached from what took place. I would rather run the other way than face reality. If there is hope for me, please give me a second chance. Can You mend this broken heart of mine?

 Thought: Where do I start in my lifestyle to walk without immorality and regain a new heart?

Reflection:

Flawless Choices of Love

Daughters of Jerusalem, I charge you: Do not arouse or awaken love until it so desires.

—Song of Solomon 8:4

My daughter, I told you I had the answers to find pleasure in loving once again, and I do indeed. The first step is to follow Me. Follow My Son, Jesus, to the cross, He laid down His life for you and gave you *perfect love*. When you come to the cross and give Me all your baggage, I begin to remove the pain that has held you captive. I will remove the self-hatred and low self-esteem, and begin to show you that in your life before Me you were sinning against yourself. You allowed others to violate you and found yourself in unhealthy relations because of these acts done to you.

I want you to learn to trust Me and *share from your heart*. I will begin to heal your heart of two; I will mend it into one for a new beginning. Your body, dear child, is the body of the Holy Spirit. He is *your comforter* and guides you in the direction to go. Do not sin any longer against your own body, for when you give your life over to Me, you become My property. You are royalty, daughter of the most High King. You are righteous and the Apple of My eye. *I will give you beauty for ashes* from your past and take away your sin, and a new life you will begin.

I will begin your new life by giving you back your dignity and self-respect. I will give you back your purity all except physically. You will begin to change your way of thinking in your attitude, and you will know who you are in Me. I will show you that when you love you, others will too. No longer hide behind a wall of shame. *Do not awaken love, My daughter, before it is time.* I have the right match for you. Do not get discouraged. Put your trust in Me. I will pour out My love on you and provide your heart with what it needs.

Prayer: God, I need You more desperately than I realize. My heart is broken in two and filled with filth from my past. Guide me and keep me strong in my moments of weakness. Cleanse me of the attitudes and carefree lifestyle I have known. Draw me to You, and show me a new road to walk. It will not be easy, though I am learning to see that nothing is impossible with You, God.

 Thought: What would it be like to have a clean heart and to begin all over from a place of purity in Spirit, mind, and soul?

Reflection:

Perfect Unconditional Love

We love because he first loved us.

—1 John 4:19

My daughter, you needed unconditional love while growing up, something you did not receive from your earthly father though you so desperately needed it. You were searching in so many areas trying to fulfill this need, which was so important, when you were a young child. As you grew, there were unspoken expectations placed upon you; you were to act a certain way and portray an image that your father would approve of. All the while, I watched you struggle. I allowed you to experience this because I would use you for My glory one day. While your heart filled with pain and tears, I was crying too, My child. I had to allow this to happen. I knew the strength you would gain through your pain, and it would be used for *My glory* and your *future*.

Through your pain you tried to become perfect, hoping to change and become the perfect golden girl for your father, seeking his love. All the while you wanted to become you, whom I had created you to be. Your earthly father told you how to dress as if you had someone to impress and taught you manners for the public to see. He was strict with your grades; the pressure brought rebellion, and you depended on him for many things. All the while, you felt responsible for the development of who you would become. Inside you wanted to be set free, yet you found yourself bound to the circumstances. You wanted to be accepted for you and not have to live up to someone else's expectations.

It seemed, at times, you weren't living up to whom your father wanted you to be. No matter how hard you tried, he wasn't satisfied deep inside; though he didn't show it, you felt it. You weren't that boy he wanted from the start. *He loved you the best he knew how.* He tried his best to show it in ways; his heart was never all there to express it in a healthy way. As your heart cried, *"Accept me for me; don't put so many unspoken demands full of subliminal pressures. I'm drowning here, can't you see?"* These were your thoughts as you hid them for none to see. You hoped no one would discover the secret—that your life was not as perfect as your parents made it out to be.

Now that you are an adult, I'm here to open up your eyes and show you the truth. *Surrender* your father totally. You needn't worry about his love any longer. Let Me be the one to love you *unconditionally*. I knew you from the moment I created you in your mother's womb. You are My precious one whom I love unconditionally. Love Me in return and *accept My free gift* to you, My Son, Jesus, who died to give you life more abundantly.

✝ **Prayer:** Thank you for accepting me for who I am and loving me unconditionally. It is through You, Lord, that I will learn how to accept myself. I now know that unconditional love makes no demands and does not try to change us. I surrender my pain to You and ask in return that You begin to show me how to love others unconditionally.

🙏 **Thought:** How can I accept God's love if I still keep the conditions of others?

🌹 **Reflection:**

Innocence Restored

I will repay you for the years the locusts have eaten-the great locust and the young locust, the other locusts and the locust swarm- my great army that I sent among you.

—Joel 2:25

Out of the depth of your pain comes the vivid memory of days gone by. The deep-rooted abuse done to you carries on inside the experience that stole your childhood innocence from you. Your frail heart was beginning to grow strong until a hand of hurt came upon it and crushed it. The growing innocent child inside became strong, yet not in a healthy manner but rather in an unhealthy one caused by the Enemy, Satan himself. Deep inside your heart is rejection—rejection from your earthly father that needs *My healing love* to be poured deep into your wounds, which are filled with hate, anger, dirtiness, and unbearable acts of torment. No daughter of mine should have to experience this kind of abuse. The evil force that came upon you was not from Me, My child.

My heart broke with anguish as I witnessed your pain. It is because of that pain that I went to the cross for you, to give you *beauty* for your pain one day. I know you are enraged; your heart is full of hate for what was done to you. The Enemy of this world comes to kill, steal, and destroy. All the while I have come to *love you and give you liberty*. Relinquish your memories to Me. Give Me the insecurities associated with the unworthiness and trauma you encountered. Allow My love to penetrate deep into your wound and begin the healing on all fronts.

I know this is hard to read as I pour out your heart back to you. There is a *healing property* that takes place when truth is revealed and dealt with. I am here, holding your hand, catching every hot, hate-filled teardrop that is released. In actuality, I feel each teardrop and begin to heal your heart in the chamber it came from. I promise that as you shed your tears you will experience a new healing you never imagined. Trust me. Your Father in heaven loves you and is beginning to heal you even now.

✠ **Prayer:** Father in heaven, I cry out to You for help. I cannot bear the pain I feel inside. It hurts so deep in my heart; I feel as if it will burst. Give me the grace I need as I relive the pain and hand it over to You.

🐾 **Thought:** Where, exactly, should I begin to unbury my pain?

🌿 **Reflection:**

At the Cross

Blessed is the one whose transgressions are forgiven, whose sins are covered.

—Psalm 32:1

As I begin to tear down the emotional wall you have built up, I will use it to help you heal from every hurt. Do not fear; let go and let Me help you heal from each hurt and pain that you have. Know that I am waiting with *loving arms to wrap around you,* ready to replace every pain and emotional scar that you have. I will replace them with a new feeling of worthiness in Me and a love that comes from Me alone. My love for you runs deep inside, and there is nothing I cannot do.

Be transparent with Me. Do not hide and hold back. Know that I am here with you, for you, to love you in a way you have never felt. I want to share with you the intimate embrace you have needed, to embrace you with a love that I desired for you to have the first time you decided to make a decision to look for love from a man. You gave yourself away, believing inside you would be fulfilled of that emptiness you felt in your heart. Though you didn't see Me as your bridegroom at the time, but just as your Father, I love you as a perfect husband loves you.

I felt your heart the first time you gave your purity away. I was there. I was watching you, knowing you would regret your decision. You had awakened love before it was time. Your act of sin brought you pain. I was loving you and forgiving you just the same. I was someone who cared and knew the outcome of your decision. I was ready to stop you, yet I did not take away your free will. I spoke to your spirit, yet you would not listen though you heard deep inside. It was that still, small voice saying, "I love you, My child. *I am with you always, even now.* You don't have to go through with this. This is not My perfect love for you." *I took your decision to the cross.* I forgave you for the choice you made even then.

Prayer: Lord, help me to remember all the times I reached for love and was not fulfilled. My heart was still empty. Bring to me stillness in my spirit and allow me to lay all my transgressions at Your feet of the cross.

 Thought: What did Jesus take to the cross for me?

Reflection:

Tainted Love

If our hearts condemn us, we know that God is greater than our hearts, and he knows everything.

—1 John 3:20

You lie there in wait for love to come, never truly getting to receive all that there is for you. You feel cheated, as the one you have poured your heart into and deepened your feelings for will never return the same deep emotion back to you. Even in your dreams I see your heartache, My child. I know the agony you have felt in dealing with the seeming unfairness of life. Why can't you have the one you are so desperately involved with, at the heart level you desire? *"What is wrong with me?"* you think. *"Why can't I have this love that should be mine?"* The reason is this, My daughter: this person does not belong to you. You were with him for a time—a season, that was all. I did My best to show you this was not the relationship for you. You were right; there was something between you and him, yet it was not him I intended for you to be with.

Your love became tainted. It was a wishful relationship, not a reality. The one you chose was not in My design. The plans I have for you are with someone else. My plans for you will go forth. Though it was hard to see you go through all you did, My ultimate purpose for your life is going forth now. Your healing is what is needed for My purpose, and it will be used for My glory. I know you can handle all things through My strength I give you. Do not discount the small beginnings. My healing touch is powerful and will heal your inner heart and comfort you in the pain you experience.

Give Me your love and all your past loves. Some are so deeply rooted you cannot remember. Allow Me to remove the hurtful memories from your past and heal them. You can trust Me, My daughter. I know what is locked deep inside your *wounded heart.* Give Me all the tainted loves and traumas that haunt you and the pain associated with each. I love you enough to be there and listen to you as you pour out your heart. *Incline your heart to Me;* My ears are ready to listen to your heart's cry. I promise to heal the pain and restore you to your rightful state of loving. I will prepare you for the plan that is yet to come. Your emotional health will be healed by My love as I pour into your aching heart the true love you are in need of. It is all in *My timing,* not yours.

Prayer: Lord, I as I pour out my heart full of broken and tainted love, please show me where the hurt began. What is the root to all the deep pain? Help me to move and to grow in Your perfect love you have waiting for me.

 Thought: If my loves have all been tainted, then what does true, genuine love feel and look like?

Reflection:

Innocent Violation Part I

So you will purge from yourselves the guilt of shedding innocent blood,
since you have done what is right in the eyes of the Lord.
—Deuteronomy 21:9

You felt like a spider's prey captured in its web, trying to escape. Every time
you tried to move, you became emotionally and mentally drained and there was
nowhere to go. You felt as though your body was slowly shutting down, while
inside you were running a mile a minute. You were being held against your will,
whether it was physically or psychologically. There was nowhere to run, it seemed,
and no one who cared.

Who was there by your side, My child, to give you the *comfort and peace* you
needed? Who was there listening to your plea? You spoke your mind. This was
not your choice. You were forced into this and violated. Your body was not your
own; others invaded and took control. Others abused you by stealing your physical
integrity as well as your conscience. You were helpless to change the predicament
you found yourself in. Everything around you was closing in. You felt powerless,
weak, and all alone in the cold, starched white room. You held on to the table and
squeezed the nurse's hand while hot, burning tears rolled down your face. The
pain you felt was like that of a suffering prey, injured for life, a casualty who had
emotionally died to the loss just experienced inside.

My daughter, there is *hope*. Let Me explain: All this pain you have gone through
will be used for good one day. I know you want to be in denial and be numb to
the experience and the loss of your child. Yes, it is a wound caused by invasion,
yet it will not go without punishment. *"Revenge is Mine,"* says the Lord of Hosts.
I will fight those battles soon. You, My child, are whom I am concerned about
now. Your innocence was viciously mistreated, and the emotional trauma you
experienced runs deep. I know that negative emotions at times arise without
warning and you want the shame and fear to disappear.

The guilt you carry inside is not for you alone. I want you to begin to give your
trauma to Me so I can set you free. You will become innocent in My sight and
be made pure and clean. Accept My Son, Jesus, and all He did for you. His
blood on the cross of Calvary removed the guilt of innocent bloodshed from the

violation to your body. He alone says, *"You are not guilty, sinless in My sight."* I will use all your innocent violations for *My divine purpose* and turn all injuries and suffering around to be used for *My glory*. There is hope; so run to Me under My wings of safety.

 Prayer: Share with the Lord your heart's cry.

 Thought: The violations against me are hard to face. Even though it is over, am I willing to release it all to God so I can begin total healing?

Reflection:

Innocent Violation Part II

And we know that in all things God works for the good of those who love him, who have been called according to his purpose.

—Romans 8:28

Do not run, and do not fear; there is nowhere to hide. What you have gone through, My beloved, will be used for *My purpose in mind.* What the Enemy meant for evil will all be used for My glory, with you being the one who *shines.* No more flashbacks with attached suffering regarding what happened in the past. All the nightmares filled with fear will now be replaced with sweet sleep. *When you lie down at night, you will not fear, for I will be there with you* until morning's light. When that time of year comes around again and it seems as if you want to block it out, face it head-on, knowing you will see your little one again.

The Enemy of your soul wants to keep you bound to the pressure put on you by others, whether the pressure is silent or known. Do not give in and feel helpless. When you give your life to Me, you have the power in Jesus' name to enjoy your life with no denial. There are no more defenses when the Enemy tries to make you feel like a causality of your past sin, for you will walk in victory in those places where you were dead inside.

When you are out shopping and see something babyish you like, do not ignore what you are feeling. Push through the uneasiness and realize those thoughts can be overcome. I am here to help you. Cry out to Me, and I will help you to the other side. My daughter, do not reach out to harm yourself by pushing down the pain or feeling as though you need relief instead. Turn to Me for the peace you are looking for. I will make your burdens light and take upon Me your shame, which I have already done. Open up to Me and be totally real. *Do not hide behind any bricks in the wall;* bust them down once and for all.

Trust Me, My child, and you will see I have created you for a purpose. I will provide you with all you need. Give Me your life and lay down all your baggage at My feet. I am a big God, and I can bear it all. *Nothing is too difficult for Me,* as you will soon see.

Prayer: God, I am listening to You speak, and I want to feel as You say. I want to be able to walk in freedom, though I know each day will be a battle in some way. From what I know so far, You fight my battles for me; You are my Lord of Hosts. I need to give my life to You, trust You, and obey You. Please continue to help me along this journey, which is not easy. Help me to knock down the bricks in my wall so I can be totally set free. I want to be used for Your purpose and glory.

 Thought: How does God take all my pain and use it for His glory?

 Reflection:

For I Am

And the Lord said, "I will cause all my goodness to pass in front of you, and I will proclaim my name, the Lord, in your presence. I will have mercy on whom I will have mercy, and I will have compassion on whom I will have compassion."

—Exodus 33:19

You cannot hide, My child, for I can see everything. I am with you everywhere you go, and I will not leave you or forsake you. Remember, I created you and know every detail about your life. There is nothing I do not know. I know your comings and goings before you even make decisions. Yet there are times you made decisions I wish you would not have made. I knew the thoughts and what was going through your mind the day you found out you were with child, for I designed for you to be pregnant. *I do not make mistakes.* Because you went against My Word and did not wait to have sex until marriage, consequences arose. I had a purpose in that plan with the decision you made also. You did not even realize that I already knew.

Yes, for at times it was not your fault; you were the victim. You were trapped and forced to surrender over to your abuser. I was with you. My grace is sufficient for you in all situations. Yes, I know, you were frightened; fear gripped your heart, and you were concerned for your life and your baby's. You or your abuser thought the situation should be dealt with by ending the life inside you. Yet never did you realize the emotional trauma it would cause one day and the unseen side effects and issues it would have on you later in life. My child, I had all these details in the palm of My hand.

I am sorry for the anguish it caused you to come to the conclusion you reached concerning your situation at hand. Your heart was consumed with fear and concern, as you felt trapped in your circumstance. Even though you felt this life to be a burden, I could see the hesitation you had to go through with it. I cried tears as you cried. My daughter, *I experienced the pain you felt.* There is nothing I have not experienced with you. I experienced all these things on the cross for you two thousand years ago, before you made these decisions.

Come, My child, pour out your aching heart and allow Me to give you rest and surround you with My *loving peace* that comes from Me alone. My *healing grace will flow over you and consume you like an* all-*consuming fire.* Surrender all the grief and shame to Me. Your healing is now beginning.

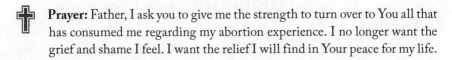 **Prayer:** Father, I ask you to give me the strength to turn over to You all that has consumed me regarding my abortion experience. I no longer want the grief and shame I feel. I want the relief I will find in Your peace for my life.

Thought: With the Lord on my side, why would I even hesitate to withhold from Him?

Reflection:

Surrendering It All

Trust in the Lord with all your heart and lean not on your own understanding; in all your ways acknowledge him, and he will make your paths straight.

—Proverbs 3:5–6

As you begin to surrender your secret to Me, My daughter, I will have you begin to search deep into your soul to see what is inside that needs to be healed. Your secret is safe with Me, for I know all things. I am here waiting for you to let go and share with Me your flaws. No one is perfect, My child, except My Son, Jesus. Because of His perfection, *you can be made whole in Him* and remain healed. He is your *Savior and Redeemer.*

The wall of denial is beginning to come down. The trauma that your abortion brought, which you were hoping to escape, has now begun to emerge, and you cannot handle it your own way. Reality has set in, and you realize that your past and pain must be dealt with. The hidden secrets that have been blocked all this time are being exposed, and healing is on its way. The hope is in Me. I alone have the power to protect you from the lies of the Enemy. Give Me each one, and I will begin to show you the truth. Begin to deal with the truth of what your mind and heart have gone through. I will cleanse you and give you in exchange a spirit of courage, love, and power, and a sound mind.

I am the one who goes before you and fights your battles. I am giving you the strength to endure emotionally the healing that needs to occur in your heart. As you begin to surrender to Me your self-hatred and bitterness that have built up over time since your abortion, *I will fill your heart with a peace and comfort you cannot describe.* My love for you is unending and abounding in grace, giving you the longing to be made whole and healed in My Son, Jesus.

In My presence is a *peace that passes all understanding.* My desire is to see you healed and walking along the path of freedom. Give to Me daily the issues and reminders from the past that haunt you. Trust in Me to guide you down a path of boldness and acceptance. In all you do, trust Me to keep your paths straight.

✝ **Prayer:** As I lay before You my past and surrender all my secrets, begin to fill me with Your presence as I go down these paths of my past to begin my healing. I know there is a peace and safety in Your midst. Please guide my tender yet calloused heart at times into a place of surrender before You.

🐚 **Thought:** Surrendering My secret will take courage. What is the roadblock from my past that is holding me back from letting it all go so I can receive a new heart and begin to walk in a straight path?

🌿 **Reflection:**

Great Exchange

Do not fear, for I have redeemed you; I have summoned you by name; you are mine. When you pass through the waters, I will be with you; and when you pass through the rivers, they will not sweep over you. When you walk through the fire, you will not be burned; the flames will not set you ablaze. For I am the Lord your God, the Holy One of Israel, your savior.

—Isaiah 43:1b–3a

When all life's questions seem to be without answers and the people around you seem not to care, reach out to Me; I'm here, waiting for you to share. Your pain is unbearable, so give it all to Me. Your actions are self-destructive, and you want to end your life because of shame and misery. You can no longer feel, and the numbness has now ingrained into your mind. My daughter, I know things seem hopeless now, but it will all change in due time. Take on *My mind*, the thoughts I have toward you. I love you despite what you have done and how bad you feel. When I am in your life, I will bring you hope and that ray of sunshine. I know the thoughts I think toward you. It is *My strength* that is made perfect in your weakness. What you are going through is all for a reason, and when I am by your side, I will give you answers and guide you to life more abundantly. I hear your thoughts repeating that you have no more hope and desire for living. You say your self-esteem was consumed by all the guilt and despair and regret from your past decisions and pain. You are ready to give up and call it a day.

Wait! Do not let go. Hold on to your life and find comfort in My Word. You may feel that there is no use, that you have tried everything. The truth is, you have not tried *My Truth, which is living and cuts like a two-edged sword*. My Son, Jesus, paid the price and bought you with His blood long ago. Your ransom has been paid, and your sins have been forgiven. There is no reason to permit the Enemy of your soul to have any more room. Because of the blood of My Son, Jesus, who took it **all** to the cross to give you everlasting life with Me, the keys of death are gone and the Enemy has no more *victory*! When you accept Me into your life, you have a second chance. Jesus bore your burdens for you and came to help make your paths straight.

The fear is gone, and the darkness of your soul is becoming light. Open up to Me and share from your heart. Give to Me the grief weighing heavy on your soul. I love you, My child, and you are worthy in My sight. *Your heart I will restore with flesh* as I take away the *calloused shell full of numbness.* No more self-punishment, for Jesus removed your regret. There is a great exchange waiting for you. I take from you your guilt, rejection, despair, and shame, and in return you receive hope, love, forgiveness, and a new life—here on earth as well as in eternity.

 Prayer: God, I want what you are sharing with me. I do not have to feel like this any longer. I really want to continue living, but not like this. You say you will take all this shame I feel, all my sins, and give me a fresh start? I do not deserve this; how can this be? I have been living in a pit of despair, and seems to have been an eternity since I last experienced freedom. I need the hope You talk about so I can begin to live once again and feel self-worth. I want a smile on my face again and lightness in my heart. Please, God, whatever it takes!

 Thought: Am I willing to give God my trauma associated with my abortion? Am I willing to pay the price to begin to walk in healing the cost?

Reflection:

Follow Me

Then he said to them all: "If anyone would come after me, he must deny himself and take up his cross daily and follow me."

—Luke 9:23

I, the Lord your God, am a jealous God. I created you to love Me, not things that cannot give you what you need. I am one who wants your *wholehearted devotion.* Pour out your love to Me; follow Me. This requires much, My child; are you ready? Are you ready to make a commitment and *surrender all* to Me? This will be a sacrifice; this you will soon see.

My daughter, what I want you to realize is that you have sacrificed all your life. You have tried to be someone or you have put on a mask for others to see you as one person, all along hiding behind your insecurities. In order to deal with your insecurities, you turn to vices to cover them up, hoping no one will find out the real you. These vices come in the form of all the addictions you have made a part of your life. Think back to the times you picked up that bottle of liquor or a bag of dope, or how about when you reached for the bottle of pills, a gallon of ice cream that you ate in one sitting, or even a razor blade. You didn't care what you were doing at the time—on the surface, that is. Yet deep inside you were crying, even screaming. After a while you become a *slave* to that which you run to. It consumes your thinking, trying to drown out the memories and the hurting heart you are carrying. Sooner or later you end up in bondage to that which you escape to.

My daughter, when you run to something other than Me, in reality it has control of you and you become its slave. The Enemy has you bound; your heart is in chains, your spirit is locked in captivity, and you are forfeiting your freedom. I have something to offer you—*total freedom in Me!* Come to Me; don't run from Me. When you make a decision to give Me your life, to surrender all over to Me—when you make Me your master—you will then experience true freedom.

Become My daughter, and you will soon see the *freedom you can experience and the beauty I will restore in your heart.* The healing will begin to take place if you give Me your all. Give to Me your past, secrets, and each addiction. When I become your Lord, you give up your rights. I am your Master, and *your identity is in Me.* Obey Me, My child, and I will help you along the journey to make things right, healing you from all your wrong choices and giving you a new life. I will give you joy, grace, and eternal life in exchange for your shame, guilt, and fear. Truly surrender and become My slave and experience true freedom, which only I can give.

 Prayer: Help me, Lord, not to continue to become a slave to my selfish pleasures and care what others think. I surrender my burdens, insecurities, and masks to You so the chains around my heart will loosen from me.

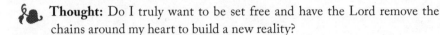 **Thought:** Do I truly want to be set free and have the Lord remove the chains around my heart to build a new reality?

Reflection:

Part II

Leaning toward the Cross while Holding His Hand

Jesus Knows

Jesus was with you in the clinic.
He was with you in the procedure room.
He was there standing next to you as
your child was being taken from within your womb.
Jesus was loving you just the same,
crying for your pain,
'cause He already took your guilt and shame
to the cross that day.
He hung there, my dear child,
giving up His life for you.
Already did He know
the choice you'd make and
what the future held for you.
With Jesus' arms stretched out,
He showed you how much He cared.
He took all your pain and suffering
in hope that your life would be spared.
As He looked out into the crowd that day,
he saw your face among many,
knowing that one day in the future
you would be on your knees, pleading.
Pleading for forgiveness for the mistake you made,
crying out to Abba Father for mercy.
And on His face that day He showed
a deep, passionate look full of loving grace.
The anguish that held your heart captive
since the day you made the choice
to end your child's life
would soon be stripped away empty
and filled with God's love in its place.
So as you get on bended knee
and ask the Lord for forgiveness,
know His loving arms are wrapped around you
as He receives you into His presence.

The Father's Heart

...being confident of this, that he who began a good work in you will carry it on to completion until the day of Christ Jesus.

—Philippians 1:6

My daughter, as I begin to walk with you on this journey, do not fear, for I am with you, say I, your Father. I am with you every step of the way. No matter how painful it may be and feel, I want you to journey down these roads. I have a plan for you. Your pain will turn into beauty and be used to bring Me glory. There is nothing I can't forgive you from. Your deepest secrets are safe with Me. I hold them in My heart for only Me to see. Nothing will I withhold from you. As you open up your heart to Me, I will pour My *loving grace and forgiveness* upon you.

Reach down deep inside and let go of the pain. Give it all to Me. Give Me the abuse you have experienced—not only the abuse you have done to yourself, but also the abuse done to you by others. My child, I love you despite all you have done. Don't you know that I created you, that I planned your days? Both good and bad I knew were going to happen. I had control even then, though I did not take away your free will. I am still a gentleman, and I love you with a father's heart. Not as your earthly father; his heart is with flaw. Yet mine is a perfect heart, full of love to accept you despite your mistakes and grievances. I love you, child, with an *everlasting love, an unconditional love.* I loved you so much in the midst of your sin that I sent My Son to die for you so you could live in eternity with Me. For without My Son, this would not be possible. Come to Me, run into My arms, and let Me shower you with love and know the grace I have for you, even when you do not deserve it.

You feel like a failure, as if you have to make up for the mistakes you made. There is nothing you can do to make it go away. You are to give Me your burdens, let Me own the pain. I took it to the cross two thousand years ago; that is how much I love you. You cannot do this on your own. I am here waiting for you. I want to reach down deep inside your heart and show you that I took your pain upon My body and it was nailed to the cross.

Though it feels like a wilderness at times, as if these feelings of pain, shame, and suffering will never go away, I am letting you know, My child, that I am the only one who can take it away. From Me you cannot hide. I live inside, waiting to be invited into your life. I won't leave. You see, you need Me, and I will cure all the poison you have allowed to consume you inside. Your past is the past. Your future is in My hands. Do not run; yet run to Me. I am waiting for you.

 Prayer: Open my heart, Lord, so I can begin to see all that I need to lay down at your feet. Help me to realize You accept and love me despite all of my past sins.

 Thought: How much of my past will I let you have, Lord?

⌘ **Reflection:**

Unforgiving Past

For if you forgive men when they sin against you, your heavenly Father will also forgive you.

—Matthew 6:14

My daughter, as you begin to let go of the layers of unforgiveness, which you have placed on top of each other over time, eventually you and I together will get to the root cause of all your pain. This process will not be easy. The deeper you go, the more painful it will be, yet the freedom I will give you is worth it all. Lay down your burdens to Me. Take the people you need to forgive and hand them over to Me. They are enemies in your past who need to be forgiven. When you *forgive*, the *shackles of bondage* will come falling off and My cleansing blood will be poured into your spirit. You will feel a weight being lifted from your heart. Your shoulders will be lighter as you give Me the load this pain of unforgiveness has caused you all this time.

As you travel down the layers and begin to remove your past choices that have been burdening you, you will experience the intensity of hurt that you have buried all this time. *Do not fear.* Let the emotions flow. Let the tears come rolling down your cheeks which have been hardening over time. You have wanted the tears to flow, yet you would stop them as they came. You didn't want to go there. The pain of the past hurt too much. Now is the time, My daughter, to let the tears fall upon your rosy red cheeks and experience the softness beginning to emerge. The transformation will happen within your heart and will overflow down your cheeks, softening with each new teardrop. As time goes on, the heat of your tears, a result of all the bitterness locked up inside, will begin to leave and your tears will become like a *cool summer rain*. A cleansing flow released by My power will liberate your emotions and allow healing and forgiveness to come forth toward your enemies.

As you *let go and release to Me the memories of hurt and feelings of tormenting pain*, I will remove the sting in your heart. No longer will the ugliness of resentment resound in your soul, which is the root cause of all your painful memories. Forgiveness does not say the trauma never took place; it simply means you surrender to Me the pain it caused, that I may heal your wounds. I will heal you spiritually and bring peace to your spirit. Forgiveness says you will not *get even* and the anger you feel will eventually subside. You do not have to reconcile with those who hurt you. I will give you a new heart for those who caused pain, and the freedom you feel will be like none other. In time your heart will be made brand-new; the closer you are to your healing, the more closure you will have.

Truly forgiving is a decision we make. Forgiveness will not be easy, and at times it may take a long while. Take My hand as I guide your steps down the path of healing I have for you. All pain will be removed, and I will make you whole. *Come walk with Me and allow Me to begin your healing journey.*

 Prayer: Lord, just thinking about beginning to face the issues surrounding my unforgiveness is unbearable. The wound runs deep, and I so much want to release it into Your hands. Know that Your presence is here. Only through Your help can I begin to do this. I give You my hand. Please help me begin to forgive so I can receive the freedom it will bring.

 Thought: What do I surrender first so my heart will begin to heal?

 Reflection:

Key to Forgiveness

Let the peace of Christ rule in your hearts, since as members of one body you were called to peace. And be thankful.

—Colossians 3:15

What do you struggle with down deep inside that has been locked, sealed, and tucked away so no one can see where the pain lies? What will it take, My child, for you to untie the past of long ago or something that may have happened recently? There is something blocking you from your healing within. Could the barrier be that one decision that needs to be made, called "forgiveness"? You ask yourself, "How can I forgive the one that hurt me the most" or "How can I forgive myself of the choices I've made?" These questions, My daughter, haunt you, I know. The answer to these questions is simple, yet quite costly and not easy to do. Let go of the unforgiveness so your freedom can begin. The chains of bondage are still upon you, until you decide to give them to Me so I can unlock each with *the key of forgiveness.*

The ability to forgive cannot be attained by you alone. My Son, Jesus, gives you the strength and grace to forgive those who have hurt you. As you begin to *surrender to Me* the unforgiveness, anger, and hurt associated with those in your abortion experience, your heart begins to be *set free*. Forgiveness is the key to the chains around your heart, which is being broken, and the weapon used to break the bondage the Enemy of your soul put there long ago. *Forgiveness equals freedom,* My child, and I will give you the strength to let go and release it to Me. As far as forgiving yourself is concerned, that cannot be done. It is I alone, the Lord your God, who can forgive you. Jesus took your abortion and *nailed it to the cross.* The trauma associated with it is gone and has been so for a very long time. You do not have the ability to forgive yourself. You are *forgiven by the blood* shed for you on the cross. Jesus *rescued you* from the lies of the Enemy and gives you a new life. For it is by My grace you have been given new life. Have the faith to believe your sins were taken upon the cross, and accept the free gift waiting for you. Accepting My forgiveness equals being released of all the guilt and shame you have carried behind your wall of denial and depression all this time.

I'm calling you, My daughter, beckoning your spirit to Mine. Stay close to My heart, My child, so the wiles of the Devil will not draw you away. The benefit of forgiveness is mainly for you. *Forgiveness* will replace the agony and sorrow and replace it with a peace that surpasses understanding, giving you unspeakable joy. My forgiveness sets you free and allows you the opportunity to *walk in love and tenderhearted mercy*. Take the new life I offer you and allow Me the opportunity to use your pain for your gain and My glory.

 Prayer: Oh Jesus, how I long to be set free and walk in peace. It is so difficult to just let go at times, because then I would be letting go of my child and the memory. Come fill me with Your presence and give me the strength and tenacity to do what You are calling me to do. Be gracious to me as the layers begin to fall away and I begin a new life with You.

 Thought: Now that Jesus has made the offer for me to accept His forgiveness and for my new life to begin with Him, am I willing to finally let go of the trauma of my abortion and give over control to Jesus?

 **Reflection:**

Your Forgiving Father

You are forgiving and good, O Lord, abounding in love to all who call to you.

—Psalm 86:5

Forgiveness is not a matter for the flesh, but a matter for the heart. It is My heart that longs for you to forgive those who have wronged you, to forgive those who were not there for you in the midst of your pain when you were crying out to someone. All along, I was there, waiting for you to look up or turn around and see Me standing there beside you. You could not physically see Me, yet My presence was ever so strong with you. I got drowned out by the shock of your discovery. You could not hear My still, small voice calling to you in the midst of your drama and confusion about what to do next. I had answers for you. I had been the one all along with plans for your life. The choices you made had consequences, and I was waiting there with the answers. Instead of seeking Me, you turned to friends or the partner who was in this with you.

The shock on your face at the result of your pregnancy test was not a surprise to Me, although it came as a surprise to you. In earlier instances, the results were relieving, yet that final test was not the answer you had hoped for. My child, I have had the answers all along. *Come back to Me.* I am *waiting.* I *forgive* you. It is because I forgive that you can forgive also. Yes, it is hard. It is especially hard when forgiveness involves those you love who are dear to your heart. Humans are not perfect; only My love for you is perfect. I forgive you; now let Me help you forgive those who hurt you.

I too had to forgive those who caused Me pain, mocked Me, and left Me to die. I took your unforgiveness to the cross and forgave you long before you even made the choice you did. To forgive is a *choice*, not an emotion. It's the choice I told My Father in heaven I would make for you long ago, before you were even born. Did I want to take all your sins upon Me and die for you? I became human and felt your pain. I realized your pain was a great burden and that you could not go through life alone.

I will become your *comfort*, the peace in your innermost being that you search for. I have not forgotten you, My child. I am here, waiting to take your burdens from you and carry them. My yoke is easy. Rest upon Me, and let Me show you how to handle unforgivness and have you release it to Me. Do not be buried any longer with the consequences of unforgivness; give them all to Me. I am waiting, dear child, My daughter whom I long to set free.

 Prayer: Open my heart and unlock the unforgivness that is still there. Help me to forgive the people who hurt me the most. Remove the ugliness and give me a clean heart, Lord.

Thought: Whom, exactly, do I need to turn over to the Lord and let go of?

Reflection:

Freedom From Forgiveness

For he has rescued us from the dominion of darkness and brought us into the kingdom of the Son he loves, in whom we have redemption, the forgiveness of sins.

—Colossians 1:13–14

You have it in your heart that you can never forgive yourself for what you have done. Yes, My child, you are right. You can *never forgive yourself* for the choice you made. It is *only I, your Heavenly Father,* your Creator, *who can forgive you*. Nothing you do will make up for the choice you made. You cannot go back in time and change the circumstances. I knew this long ago, and that is why it is through *My Son, Jesus,* you have been forgiven. He is your *redemption*. He is your answer to all your pain. He is the one who gives you a *saving grace and a new life in Him*. His death on the cross was the ultimate sacrifice for your mistake and will give you the freedom and peace you are searching for.

Accept My love for you, daughter, My precious one and apple of My eye. My Son, Jesus, took the lies you believed, and each was nailed to the cross with Him. It is I who gives you *everlasting life*. Receive My forgiveness. I paid for your sin so you did not have to take the penalty of death. I gave you life on the cross that day. Reach out and touch Me; *I'm right beside you*. I have never left you. It was the Enemy who had you stray from the truth you knew deep inside. This truth has had you hiding all this time. Give Me the anger you feel toward yourself. Give Me the bitterness you hold toward others, which it seems has been buried for an eternity.

I am the light your heart needs inside to heal and forgive what others have done to your life. Hand all of the stubbornness over to Me so I can fill you with *My forgiving and loving grace*. I will help guide you and show you how to repay evil with love and bondage with freedom.

Prayer: I surrender to You, my stubbornness Lord, which is probably the very thing standing in the way of my forgiveness toward others. I want to receive Your forgiveness for my sins. The pain reminds me of what has been done to me and what I have done to myself. Guide me to the cross, where my victory and forgiveness lie. It is Your Son, Jesus, I so long to have in my life.

 Thought: Jesus emptied Himself on the cross that day for me. What is holding me back from doing the same before Him so I can receive the freedom waiting for me?

Reflection:

One by One

Come to Me, all you who are weary and burdened, and I will give you rest.
—Matthew 11:28

My daughter, you feel as if there is no hope, as if you're in bonds and chains up to your throat. The hidden secret that covers you with guilt and shame begins to overtake you, until one day you cannot hold this burden in any longer. The weight upon your shoulders, the pain deep in your heart, is too heavy to hold on to any longer. Your heart is sinking in sin because of the choice you made. Before you suffocate and drown, lay down those burdens and give them to Me. There is no sin I will not forgive you of.

I will wipe away the sin in your life with My Son's blood, which He shed for you on the cross. The stain, the memory, of what you chose to do will always be there. Yet I can help you to make your burden light. I will begin to help you heal with those feelings left behind. Will it be easy, My child? No, I'm afraid not. Allow Me to have the shame, guilt, grief, anger, control, fear, and hate and help you heal by putting these issues to rest in their right place, one layer at a time. Together we will deal with the aftermath of your choice.

The choice you made, the sin you committed to end your child's life, has been forgiven and wiped away and is no more. What you need to deal with is the in between. Accept the fact these issues are a result of your choice. My grace I give you will help you get through the deep feelings daily as you relinquish your hold on them and accept *My loving grace.*

My child, what once to you represented a painful event in your life, an event buried deep inside, your hidden secret, will one day soon be let out, and you will be set free. The choice you made to end your child's life and how you felt afterward will be looked upon differently. I know it is hard to grasp, yet this will be your new reality once you have been set free. What once was covered with shame, guilt, and fear will be replaced with acceptance, unconditional love, and grace by Me. This will happen when you let go and let Me have control.

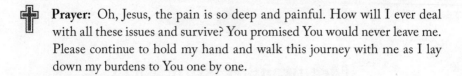

Prayer: Oh, Jesus, the pain is so deep and painful. How will I ever deal with all these issues and survive? You promised You would never leave me. Please continue to hold my hand and walk this journey with me as I lay down my burdens to You one by one.

Thought: Am I willing to let the Lord have every aspect of my abortion and begin my healing?

Reflection:

Mountain of Light Part I

I waited patiently for the Lord; he turned to me and heard my cry. He lifted me out of the slimy pit, out of the mud and mire; he set my feet on a rock and gave me a firm place to stand.

—Psalm 40:1–2

My daughter, I see the state of mind you are in—one of confusion and not knowing which way to turn. It seems as though all of life is closing in on you and you want to start all over. You wish this weren't really happening. You cannot seem to catch your breath as life closes in around you. The emotions you are feeling are consuming your entire being, pulling you down into the pit of despair, never ending. Your mind races to the past, and darkness consumes every opening of light it passes by. You want to reach up and cease all this pain; you have tried, and as you do, you are getting smothered with all the shame that has come your way.

Every positive thought you once claimed as a part of your life has now been filled with hopeless despair, and it seems Death is knocking on your door. You are in bondage, My child, and have no more strength. The Enemy of your soul has instilled chains of lies in place of your strength—the lies of this world concerning the baby you conceived. It was not a blob of tissue, as you were led to believe. Negative emotions entered your mind, and in the midst of your fear your vision became impaired. The truth was blocked out, and you began to sink into a pit of deep depression, where you could not breathe.

Do not grow weary, for there is always hope and a new beginning. You need to reach up and look to Me. Allow Me to give you what you need. *It is My strength that gives you new life and liberty.* Take hold as I reach out to you. Grab hold of *My comforting hand,* and I will pull you out and give you a firm foundation on which to stand.

Prayer: Jesus, help me please. I cry out to You in desperation. I feel as if I cannot breathe. All of who I am is reaching out to You so I can have a new beginning and a fresh start in life. I know that with You I have hope and it is Your strength I receive to go through my healing journey with You.

 Thought: If I do not reach out to the Lord for help, will I ever get my healing? Also, what steps am I willing to take to regain my strength?

Reflection:

Mountain of Light Part II

You turned my wailing into dancing; you removed my sackcloth and clothed me with joy, that my heart may sing to you and not be silent. O Lord my God, I will give you thanks forever.

—Psalm 30:11–12

Daughter, how long do you plan on staying in the pit of depression which the Enemy led you into? Are you ready to get out and *be set free* to go *claim your victory*, which has been waiting for you? Are you ready to take on the mind of Christ? I want you to have mental victory as well as emotional victory. The Enemy has held you captive far too long. I'm here to give you *insurmountable joy* deep within. No more silence. Give Me your mouth so you can begin your praise and thanksgiving to Me. Step out in faith and watch Me *transform your life.*

Spend time with Me and read My love letter to you, the Holy Scriptures. There you will find answers to your questions and find the blessings I have for you. Do not keep silent any longer and drown in your misery. My hand is upon your head, My daughter, ready to scoop you out of the pit of the miry clay. I will give you strength as eagles' wings and carry you until you can firmly plant your feet on the ground. I am your anchor and will guide you through the storms as they come. Trust Me and see that I am good. I will remove the despair from your life and clothe you with joy. I'll take your pain and replace it with healing and pleasure. I will exchange your shame for blessing and restore your self-image in who you are in Me. I will do away with self-punishment and secure you with loving yourself. I will erase your embarrassment and give you the grace to face what is ahead of you. It is through Me, My daughter, that you have your being and are healed from all your trespasses. *I remove your sins and remember them no more.*

I will *put a new song in your heart and turn your sorrow and mourning into dancing.* Put your total trust in Me. You have nothing to fear, for I am your *shield and buckler*; I go before you in battle and will fight for you. No longer will depression consume you and be a part of your life. Set your mind on things above that are pure and lovely, trustworthy, and of good report. I will lead you out of darkness and into the light of My glory, blessing you, as your heart is full of thankfulness and praise.

✝ **Prayer:** I want this joy You speak of. I want to be set free and be who You have created me to be. I extend my hand out to You, for I am ready to walk in victory. Remove from me what hinders my walk with You. I will praise You and thank You for my healing and give You glory for the changes in my life.

🐾 **Thought:** What am I going to do differently than what I currently do, to change my way of thinking as well as my actions so they will follow suit and depression will leave?

❧ **Reflection:**

Expecting Heart

I am worn out from my groaning. All night long I flood my bed with weeping and drench my couch with tears.

—Psalm 6:6

I hear your heart crying out of deep desperation as you immerse yourself physically in your sorrow from within. I see the pain you are displaying in ways others cannot see. I feel the emotional anguish beckoning to be discovered while all along you are trying to hide it from the everyday crowd. I sense the mental torment you are in, trying to act normal from day to day. I know your every thought, every memory, and every wound, My child. Your wounds run deep, though not many can see your suffering spirit and anguished soul, which have been a part of you for quite a while. Pour out your tears and weep. I collect them all and feel your pain. Be honest with Me and give Me it all. There is nothing I cannot handle. I have endured it all. Allow the tears to flow like a deluge of turbulent water, cascading down into a waterfall, gushing into a pool of water that overflows into a tranquil lake. The calm lake represents *My Holy Spirit, your Comforter.*

I feel each teardrop that flows into the calmness of My Holy Spirit. I hear the cries and prayers you lift up to Me. As you cry out for mercy, My hands extend to you *forgiving grace*; they will remove your *misery* and replace it with *hopefulness* and provide for you My *loving mercy* in exchange. I took your misery, abuse, and excruciating distress to the cross and bore your pain and mistreatment. I was persecuted for living a life doing as My Father called Me to, full of no shame. Yet I took your shame to the cross that day. I grieved and agonized, knowing the procedure you would one day be a part of; because of your decision, I hung on the cross in your place. I took the torment so you would be able to walk in freedom for eternity.

Daughter, I love you, and I would have gone to the cross if you were the only lost and hurting soul. My love for you is *great and never ending*. Pour out your affliction to Me and accept My love so it can consume your aching heart.

Prayer: Father, as I pour out my aching heart to You and give to You all of the agony, I ask You to come rescue me before the tears overtake me. Hear my prayers Dear Lord as I weep in pain. Please see the condition of my mind and give me relief. Shower me with Your peace and comfort, which I know come only from You.

Thought: As I pour out my heart to the Lord, what do I want Him to exchange for my pain within?

Reflection:

Deep Within

When anxiety was great within me, your consolation brought joy to my soul.

—Psalm 94:19

It is in My presence that you become free. It is My spirit that gives you the strength to do what I have called you to do. Do not give up by looking at the circumstances around you, My child. I have known you from the beginning of time. I have always been here with you. I have a purpose in all I have you experience. The pain you feel is real. Realize I am allowing this for My glory. One day I will use your pain to *touch others*.

The situations you found yourself in were made by your choices. Yes, you made a wrong turn. I was always there, guiding you, yet your will took over and led you down the wrong path; thus you found yourself where you did. You were pregnant, full of pain and shame, feeling lost and alone. I was there all along, with *My outstretched arms* waiting for you to run into them, waiting for you to follow your heart, knowing this child was a gift from Me to you.

As you step back into the past and heal from your pain, beginning to deal with the anger others caused you, realize it is your choice what you do with that pain. Don't hold on to it; give it to Me. Now render to Me your burdens so I can *set free the pain* and it can leave once and for all. *All things are possible.* Cast your anxiety on Me and allow Me to show you who you are in Me. I have known you from the beginning of time; I have been here waiting for this day. My love for you has only grown deeper as the years of hurt have grown. Allow Me to comfort you and remove the pain you feel. Show Me all of your cuts that run deep. You hoped they would bring you comfort and get rid of the pain. But nothing can relieve your pain, My daughter—*only My love*, which covers the entirety of hurt and shame.

Permit Me to take each ounce of hurt and soothe your inner being and show you *My healing light and peace within*. I have enough love for you; My presence will always be with you. Your heart will be filled with the love of My Son, who died on the cross for you and has already taken all the shame you feel. Trust Me, My child, My way is light. Allow Me to heal those cuts and wounds. In time you will be used for *My glory to bring peace and comfort to others*.

Prayer: Lord, once again I cry out to You and ask for help with this pain I feel deep within my closed wounds. Please help me to open these wounds up, deal with all the infection inside, and receive Your healing touch upon my heart.

Thought: How deep can my cut of pain go before Jesus will rescue me?

Reflection:

Am I Walking in Peace?

Cast all your anxiety on Him because He cares for you.

—1 Peter 5:7

Do you not trust Me with your cares, My daughter? Are the stressors of life weighing you down? Is not your heart heavy enough, filled with burdens of your past mistake and all it encompasses? Is not your heart laden down with the pain you have stuffed deep inside? What have you done with the worries? Are you wearing them on the outside? You do not have to go through this anxiety any longer. Your panic attacks and nervousness you feel are real, caused by your lack of trust in Me at times. *I have come to heal and to give you a peace that surpasses all understanding.* Your burden may be weighing heavy on your heart now; however, I can lift your cares from you and give you the tranquility and security you need. *I will make your burdens light.*

It is through My action of love on the cross that I bore all your burdens, My daughter. The bondage you feel you are locked in and can't escape from has already been released, and you are free to walk in victory. There is one condition in order to receive this liberty waiting for you. My princess, you must admit you need My help and lay your cares and afflictions at My feet of the cross, allowing Me to lighten your hardship of life. Submit all your anxiety to Me, and *I will bear all tribulation for you.*

I am ultimately in control of all circumstances. *You must humble yourself* and hand over your worries and pressure to Me. I will give you the peace in your spirit that you need to go through each day with strength. For it is My strength that fills your being. I will carry the burden for you as you walk through the trials, for I am with you always. I will guard your heart and keep it from harm. Walk in peace, and feel the love in your heart I give you daily.

✝ **Prayer:** My heart is so heavy with sadness and regret; I wonder why I even had to go through all the pain I experienced. The pressure of life overwhelms me, and I feel I can't breathe at times and want to call it quits. Show me how to submit and give You my burdens.

🐚 **Thought:** What is the cost of letting go of past burdens in order to walk in the path of peace?

🌹 **Reflection:**

Will I Walk in Peace?

Be careful, or your hearts will be weighed down with carousing, drunkenness and the anxieties of life, and that day will close on you suddenly like a trap.

—Luke 21:34

My daughter, you have been given a choice in life. You are now at a crossroads in your journey of healing from your past. I have come so that you can live life and live it abundantly. You no longer have to carry the burdens of your past. Surrender the worries to Me. *I will walk each trial with you.* I will guide your every step as you humble yourself and allow Me to continue to heal you and you claim your victory.

I want you to receive *unspeakable peace* from Me; I have it waiting for you. It is a peace that surpasses all understanding. However, this is available to you at any moment in time when life seems to get hectic and your heart begins to weigh heavy. Be careful you do not go back to your old ways to escape looking for a quick a fix to relieve the pain. The only way to heal and move on in life is to go through the pain. Reach out to Me for *security,* and *stand firm* on what I am asking you to do. Look up to Me and have faith that I have you in the palm of My hand. Trust Me with your secrets and pain. Give each of them to Me so I can give you the peace your heart longs to feel.

When stressors come into your life and the past raises its ugly head, lift your head up to Me and ask Me for that peace I have for you to become reality. Turn over the anxieties to Me so the fears of your life will not consume you and your own self-will tries to gain ground. These parts of your nature have been set free in My Son's name. It is through Him you can be *transformed and changed.*

✝ **Prayer:** I know that as the pain that has been locked away for some time begins to emerge, I will need your guidance. Please equip me, Lord, with the strength to go forth and begin my healing. Shed Your light on my path to victory as I begin walking in supernatural peace. I know my healing is in Your hands, and I will begin to trust you as I hand over each part of my past to You.

🐞 **Thought:** When issues of my ugly past emerge, how will I respond so I can walk in the peace that the Lord promises?

✿ **Reflection:**

Key to Walking in Peace

Do not be anxious about anything, but in every situation, by prayer and petition, with thanksgiving, present your requests to God.

—Philippians 4:6

There is one important key that you will need to take hold of to unlock the anxiousness of life you feel. The cure to your anxiousness in life is the answer needed for all of life's issues. Once you have this core principle as part of your firm foundation in your walk with Me, you will have the *peace that surpasses all understanding.*

Prayer is the answer to peace—my peace, which I will give to you. Prayer is the solution to your anxiety, which weighs you down in the stressors of life. If you give Me your cares, I will guide you on how to walk daily, living with Me and becoming My friend. I want a relationship with you, My daughter. I created you for a purpose and I will use all your pain and worries for My glory and gain. As you draw closer to Me, I will guard your heart and strengthen you. You must trust Me to take your problems and turn them into good. I will give you the grace you need to strengthen your spirit when life's challenges come your way. You will also receive My mercy during the times of your mistakes. I took your punishment on the cross so you could walk in peace.

Spend time talking to Me. Tell Me what you want and need. Though I know all things, I want you to be a part of the victory you walk in. What are your requests, My daughter? What is on your heart? As I begin to answer your prayers, thank Me for answers yet to come as if you have already received them. This alone will bring you to a place of walking in peace with Me. Do not despise small beginnings. Each moment you spend with Me is blessed, and you will feel later as if it were an eternity. Simply put Me first in all you do, and do not be anxious about the outcome. Bring to Me all your requests, and thank Me for the answers. In doing so, the peace of God will guard your heart and mind in My Son, Jesus.

Prayer: Thank you, Lord, for Your guidance on how to walk in peace. Thank you for the grace You give me to get through each day. I know I need to lay down to You all my worries of life, to surrender them to You. I need to make You Lord of my life and trust You that Your strength will guide me daily. Your peace is what I long for.

 Thought: How will it feel to live worry free, to trust the Lord for His strength to see me through the challenges of life?

 Reflection:

Merciful God

The Lord has heard my cry for mercy; the Lord accepts my prayer.
—Psalm 6:9

I witness your petitions, My child, as you unload your agonizing heart, full of remorse and pain. I understand the rejection that has held you captive for all this time. You have waited to be set free from the bondage of an unspoken entity that has invaded your life. Your cry of heartache wrenches My Spirit, as I know that release is what your heart desires. The silent sorrow is more than you can handle at times; you feel as if you will collapse in hopelessness at any moment. Yet My strength has kept you together and has not allowed you to give up. I hear your plea of *forgiveness*. I see your broken and contrite heart before Me. Your pain does not go unnoticed as you search deep for answers to soothe the agony and bring comfort to your soul.

The choices you have made deserve to be punished. However, My Son, Jesus, terminated your sin on the cross and gave you forgiveness. Your *cry for mercy is a sweet aroma* to My nostrils, and I am attentive to your cry. You have been released from all your past mistakes, and I will answer your petition for mercy freely. You have been found with favor and pardoned from your sins. What My Son, Jesus Christ, did on the cross cements it all, for as He said, "It is finished."

I am a *merciful God* who will pour out *My loving grace* upon you. Accept My forgiveness and sin no more. You are not perfect, My child. *Remember that where sin abounds, love abounds.* Come to Me quickly and lay your sin at My feet; ask for forgiveness, and My mercy is there for you to receive. Ask for a pure heart before Me and claim your salvation and way of escape from your enemies.

Prayer: Jesus, I want peace. My heart cries in anguish for all I have done. When I look back, at times, to the sins I've committed, I can't bear the thought of what I have done. I broke Your heart, and on the cross Your Son hung for my mistakes, which He did not deserve to take. My heart cries out, and I now know You are for real. You are the everlasting God, the great I AM, which I have now begun to experience on this journey of healing.

 Thought: I have trouble confronting all my sins I have committed. What would it feel like to be Jesus, having taken on all humans' sins and never complaining? That is never-ending merciful love!

 **Reflection:**

My Blood Saves

In Him we have redemption through His blood, the forgiveness of sins, in accordance with the riches of God's grace that He lavished on us. With all wisdom and understanding,

—Ephesians 1:7–8

My daughter, the blood which was shed on the cross at Calvary saves you, redeems and forgives you. It frees you of all the bondage the Enemy Satan has so entangled you with. My blood forgives you of all your past situations and choices that you have come to the conclusion will forever be a part of your life to haunt you. I have forgiven you, My child. I paid the price for your freedom when I was nailed to the cross for your sins before you were ever even born. *I redeemed you and called you by name. My blood* was the *sacrificial cost* for your life. I was willing to lay My life down for you to give you eternal life because I have plans for you. I came and lived for you, died for you, so that in exchange you could be used by Me for My glory to shine in your life, to be a testimony of the saving power you have in My name—**Jesus**. My light in your life is what I give you daily. My blood gives you a relationship with your Heavenly Father. You were once unclean, unworthy, covered with sin from your past mistakes. When you receive Me as your savior, you are then clothed with righteousness and there is no longer guilt and condemnation in Jesus the Son. *Your past is covered and forgiven and remembered no more,* as far as the East is from the West.

I have plans for your life. I will use your story as a testimony for *My glory*. Others will be healed as you begin to share what I have done in your life. I gave you the boldness you need when I created you in your mother's womb. You have been called for a purpose, and as you surrender your life over to Me, I will guide you every step of the way. *My blood is more powerful* than you will ever know. Know that I have you in the palm of My hand and all that I have called you to do will come about in due time.

First, give Me your fears, give Me the pain and hidden secrets no one else sees except Me. I am here to shower you with My love. My love for you is My blood poured out for you on the cross and the power it instills in you. *My grace is sufficient for you.* You are My child, and My Spirit lives within you. When you surrender all to Me and I fill you with power and grace, your sin is gone. Remember, My burden is light. I know where you came from and will guide you on your journey of healing and complete victory!

 Prayer: Father, thank you for Jesus' blood and the power it brings to my life. I know that through it I have power to do what You have purposed in my life to do. Thank you once again for Your powerful, saving blood and for using me for Your glory. Continue to walk me down the journey of healing and all that You have for me.

 Thought: How can my story make a difference in someone else's life?

Reflection:

Living Water

Whoever believes in me, as scripture has said, rivers of living water will flow from within them.

—John 7:38

It is I who gives you the feeling of freedom, for I came to set the captive free when I hung on the cross for you. *I am the freedom* you gain. It is My death that gives you life eternally with Me. Do not fear or doubt the past. Let go of the emotions you have had buried alive down deep in your soul for so long. Allow Me to break the chains that have held you captive for so long. Know that I am here with you now, waiting to set you free. As you begin to relive the experience of your child's death, go to the place you have kept secret for so long. You need to encounter each of these emotional experiences once again. Only this time *I will be by your side, holding your hand, helping you* work out each one in your heart so I can heal you down deep from your hidden past.

Think back to when you made the final decision to abort. Your baby was real, alive in you and created by Me. Your child took your form and was created for My purpose. My daughter, get back in touch with that first time you found out you were with child. *Allow your spirit to grieve.* Allow the guilt and shame you have been stuffing inside for so long to come pouring out. Feel the warm tears flow down your red cheeks of heartache. Allow the roots that hold all your hurt and grief come sprouting out and flowing into My hands. I will catch each tear. It is not in vain that you go through this. Your circumstance will be used for My glory. It is your healing that needs to takes place, and when that occurs, these tears will come rushing out like geysers. The pressure of all these tears has been building up, ready to explode. Once a teardrop forms in your eyes, this will be like a wellspring of living water rushing from the deep. All the *feelings buried alive* will come to life once again in the light, no longer hidden by the darkness of your secret past and shame. All the living water will bring you peace and insurmountable joy.

There is a freedom, and in it is the cleansing from deep inside that I begin to have take place. My child, come to Me on bended knee; fall before Me and allow the hot tears to stream down your face, and My *loving arms* will wrap around you. My sleeves will wipe away your tears. Come to Abba Father. I love you, My daughter, and remember no more your painful past. It is forgiven. *My living water has healed you,* My daughter.

✠ **Prayer:** Oh Jesus, my loving Father, You know my every thought and all that I buried deep inside. Help me with Your strength to pull out the roots one by one and see Your grace on my life as the tears cleanse me from my past and give me Your healing presence.

🐾 **Thought:** Am I willing to dig deep inside so the living water of joy and healing can come rushing out?

🌿 **Reflection:**

Healing Water

Deep calls to deep in the roar of your waterfalls; all your waves and breakers have swept over me.

—Psalm 42:7

As I cleanse you of your past and what is left to be healed, it is as if I am *humbling Myself to you* in your life. I am *purging you* of all impurities left from your past. The shame is gone; the guilt is no longer part of you. You need to experience the grief so you can grieve your child's death once and for all. *Surrender to Me* all your pain, My child. I am here, loving you just the same as I did yesterday, and I will continue to love you tomorrow. I wash away the doubt; I wash away the denial and wash away the hurt that has been done to you. The memory may still be there, yet I remove it with *My loving hands* and wipe away the tears of pain. Humble yourself, My child, and let Me have it all. Dig deep into the crevice and be free from the hard, crusted mud that holds you down.

Imagine a large bowl of warm water and your feet over the top of it. As your feet are drawn to the water, it is I that washes your feet, My daughter. My water is cleansing. The healing power is in the water that flows across your ankle and cleanses you from the inside. *I have the living water that heals on the inside.* It is not the water you physically use; it is a spiritual cleansing that comes from time with Me as you surrender all you have over to Me so I may wash you clean.

This is humility in its truest form. Be receiving of what I have for your heart. Allow the healing to begin and flow deep into the areas of your heart you still need to surrender. All is Mine, because I made all of you. I created you for *My glory.* The people I put in your path to help you heal from your abortion hold My anointing, the anointing I want you to receive. This is the anointing of a servant, a lover of My Word, one who is compassionate and loving. Humbling and cleansing are the tears you shed as I catch each one in My bottle just for you.

Prayer: Jesus, as I think of You humbling Yourself for me and all You took upon your body for me, I can hardly breathe. I deserve the punishment, not You, my God of creation. You are more than words can express. Inside I am at a loss for words when I step back and realize all You took to free me from the death of my own sins. As I surrender ALL to You, I lift up my hands in humble adoration and sincere gratitude for loving me when I was unlovable. Your mercy amazes me, and it endures forever. Wash me; make me clean before your eyes, dear Jesus.

 Thought: How can I hold back when Jesus took it all for me? Will I take the first step and surrender it all to Jesus and humble myself before Him?

 Reflection:

Sincere Cleansing

Then I acknowledge my sin to you and did not cover up my iniquity. I said, "I will confess my transgression to the Lord," and you forgave the guilt of my sin.

—Psalm 32:5

As you confessed your sins to Me, I heard every one, my child. I have not forgotten you. I've been here waiting all along for you to pour out your heart to Me. I sincerely see your broken heart and the emotional trauma that runs deep to the core of your being, which centers on the abuse and shame you had been given. The shame is not from Me, My daughter; yet My Son, Jesus, took all of the bondage and shame to *the cross*. When you sincerely give Me your life, then I will come in and make your heart brand-new. I will *remove the stony, calloused shell* and remove the hurts you have held for so long.

My daughter, I want to take the chains the Enemy placed on you so long ago and set you free, *no longer bound to your past*. The memories that you have held on to for so long are gone. They are part of an old life, a life that no longer exists. Only the memories and emotions are left, and these, My child, will soon be used for My glory. You are a child of the Most High King. Your life belongs to me, Abba Father, and the great I AM. I had My Son take your transgressions to the cross, and His blood washed you as white as snow. No looking back; just look forward to the new life you will have in Him.

✝ **Prayer:** Lord Jesus, son of the Most High, thank you for taking my sins to the cross so I might have life abundantly. Forgive me of all my wrongdoings and see my heart. Remove from my core the trauma and replace it with Your compassionate love. Remove the memories that hold me in bondage, and set me free once and for all.

🐾 **Thought:** Once the Lord removes the core of my trauma, do I promise not to return to it and in doing so move forward?

🌹 **Reflection:**

Grieving Heart

Blessed are those who mourn, for they shall be comforted.
—Matthew 5:4

Daughter, I see your sorrowful heart full of loss and despair. Deep inside there is a longing to take back what you just gave up. Please be at peace knowing your child is with Me in heaven, safe in My arms waiting for you. The feeling inside your aching heart will not go away immediately. You need to grieve your loss and begin your healing. Give to Me your heartache. Nothing is too difficult for Me to handle. I am here; pour out your heart to Me. Come before Me broken with a *contrite heart*; weep the tears of anguish before Me. I am here, waiting to restore your loss with hope and peace for your future. I have plans for you and long to share them with you, My child.

The first step is to realize you cannot fill the void of loss and pain with another child. You need to grieve your loss and be healed and made whole. Maybe you have multiple losses to grieve; *each one needs special recognition of its own.* You need to grieve and bring closure and healing to your heart and its loss. Do not lose faith; *trust in Me* says the Lord. I know you went into denial, hoping all would be okay. You justified it as the right decision, and those around you knew what was right. You trusted them. Afterward your heart ached deep inside. You wore a mask to hide the truth from others. It is now the time to tear away the mask and face reality. This memory will not fade away. Lay it in My arms as you did your child.

I have had your child with Me from the moment you walked into that cold, starched white room. As your child's spirit went into My hands, *My arms went around you* to comfort you and reassure you I have been here all along. I took your losses and gave you life for eternity. Daughter, I took your decision to have a life aborted to the cross before I even held your child in My arms. I am the Creator. There is nothing I do not know. I am the *giver of life,* and each life I create has a purpose at time of conception. My plan will go forth. Give Me your heart, and I will show you the plans I desire for you.

✝ **Prayer:** Jesus, from all I have learned so far about Your nature, Your acts of kindness amaze me. You truly do care about what happens to me and were willing to take my mistakes and sins upon Your life. I am the one who deserves punishment, not You. As I mourn my child's life, continue to stay by my side and help me to grieve, releasing all the sorrow I hold inside.

🐣 **Thought:** I truly want to break down all the barriers and grieve my child's loss. When I do begin to grieve, do I have the courage to take off the mask and see reality? Why?

� **Reflection:**

Chains Broken by Love

Then you will know the truth, and the truth will set you free.

—John 8:32

A choice, My child, was made to end your child's life for one purpose only—to hide your pregnancy and keep it silent. However, in reality, after the procedure was finished, you had yet the same secret to be kept hidden once again, with more pain and shame attached this time. It was now a wound that would ever be a part of your life, being pushed deep into the valley of remorse and embarrassment, full of secrecy just the same. You felt lost and alone in this darkness that covered your heart, and you tried to escape in your own ways. You reached out for comfort, filling the emptiness you held inside with booze, drugs, food, or sex, trying to end the pain. And the result of your escape was more *heartache.*

Up until now you have been bound by the lies the Enemy has tormented you with. In your silence, those chains have become tighter as time has slipped by, while all along you have been waiting for the day to be unlocked and able to live in freedom, putting behind you the distress and defeat you once held inside. The Enemy of your soul tormented you with lies for so long they have become a part of your belief system; nonetheless, there is a way of escape. There is a secret to unlocking the silence and to beginning your healing: *My love letter to you.* This is a book you may know of, one that has not been in your possession for a while. My comforting words will bring you answers and show you how much I loved you before the age of time.

My truth will set you free. My love *covers the multitude of your sins, and the blood of My son, Jesus, forgives you; He shed that blood on the cross long ago for you.* It is His blood that washes the shame of your past away. Healing begins when the light covers the shadows and secrets are revealed. As you surrender your past, My healing touch begins to comfort your heart. The pain locked within your heart will commence to come out. Surrender to Me all you have, and allow Me to use your pain to start the healing process in others with the same wounds as you. *Your painful experiences are not in vain.* Establish this healing journey of freedom with Me now. I am here, waiting to hold your hand and walk with you. I will not leave you. I am with you always.

Prayer: Lord, as You begin to unlock my heart and I surrender to You all my pain from the past, strengthen me in spirit, and please let me feel Your presence. I am weak, and it will be Your love that gives me the strength to walk down a painful past. Break the chains with Your love as You fill my life with hope and a future full of freedom in You.

 Thought: How has living with your secret affected your ability in life to walk in freedom and victory?

�֍ **Reflection:**

Loving Exchange

...he has sent me to proclaim freedom for the prisoners and recovery of sight for the blind, to release the oppressed,

—Luke 4:18b

You cry out to Me, and I listen. You share your heart loudly and wonder if I hear you, when all along I am right beside you. I hear you, My daughter, and I'm not going anywhere. I see the pain you are going through, and I know the insecurity you feel. I know you wonder if you are worth anything and if anyone could love you as you are. You are torn apart inside. The abuse and pain that were brought to you were uncalled for; they were not of Me. I'm sorry, My daughter, for the abuse you had to endure. Let Me love you and open up your eyes, that you may see yourself as someone genuine and valuable not only to Me but also to others who are willing to share with you their testimony. I have plans for your hurt and the traumas you have experienced.

The first thing you need to do is trust Me. It is My spirit that lives inside when you accept Me as your father. I will love you the way your earthly father should have. I will meet the needs you always wanted but were scared inside to ask for. *Allow Me to open up your heart.* Visualize all you went through, little by little. Give Me your heart, and I will make it brand-new. I will put inside a *peace that surpasses all understanding.* I will fill it with a love that surpasses all others. The trauma will be washed away by My blood. The victim's way of thinking will be removed from your mind. Your thoughts will be pure, and you will be made as white as snow.

I see you as beautiful, as worthy, and as My princess. Your heart's desire is My present to you. Follow Me and obey My commands, which are to keep you protected. I will replace the trauma with the desires of your heart. *Believe on Me.* I believed on you two thousand years ago when I took your sins and trauma to the cross.

✝ **Prayer:** Father, thank you for Your willingness to take away my trauma and shame. My heart is full to abundance. I want to feel the freedom and be totally healed.

🦋 **Thought:** What will my heart feel like empty of bondage and full of loving peace?

❧ **Reflection:**

I Took It Once and for All

For God so loved the world that He gave His one and only Son, that whoever believes in Him shall not perish but have eternal life. For God did not send his Son into the world to condemn the world, but to save the world thru him.

—John 3:16–17

My child, look at all you have done and all the wrong choices you have freely made. Think back to all the pain you experienced during the time in your life when you were running scared. Many times you were living two lives and no one knew except you, or so you thought. Yet while you were in the midst of your pain and trauma, I had *already forgiven you.* I took your sins to the cross two thousand years ago. The pain you feel now is nowhere near what it could be. My Son took the pain you feel to the cross because He loved you that much even then. His blood was shed to cover all your sins you will ever commit in a lifetime, all at once on the cross. Nothing can compare to the agony and abuse He took for all humankind. His love is endless. Even if you were the only one on this earth, He would have sacrificed His life for you. His love for you runs that deep. Do not discount the things you have done. Give every single ounce of pain, trauma, and abuse you have experienced, even the pain from not keeping your child. *Jesus took that to the cross and nailed it for all eternity.*

My child, I knew ahead of time the decision that would be made. For this reason, I knew I would need to send My one and only Son to die and take your place as the Sacrificial Lamb, *cleaning you of your sin and making you as white as snow.* He did this so you would not have to pay the ultimate penalty for your sin. My Son, Jesus, did that for you. The penalty you have had to carry around all this time is your hidden, secret sin and your inability to talk about it. You have had to carry with you the shame the Enemy has put you under, carrying the burden for all this time and locked in bondage. It is over! *Jesus paid the price for you.* He is the one that took your suffering. *His forgiving grace and mercy* are what you need. His *cleansing blood* runs through you to make you as white as snow, cleansing you from all unrighteousness.

Come to Me, and I will wrap *My loving arms around your aching heart* and the pain you feel. I will release inside a *pure love* that can come only from Me. Give

Me your heart, give Me your sins, and give Me all the pain and abuse inside. I'm here waiting. My Son thought of you on the cross, knowing you could not bear the pain for eternity. Let go once and for all and allow the freedom I have for you to *consume* your spirit. The chains are off; the shackles have been unlocked. You are no longer bound by your past. I have set you free. Come to Me, My daughter. I welcome you to your new family. I am your Heavenly Father, and I am your Abba Father.

✝ **Prayer:** (In your own words, ask Jesus Christ to be the Lord and Savior of your life, and surrender all to Him. If you already are a Christian, take this time to ask the Lord to heal you and give you the peace you long for. Ask for His forgiveness, and accept what He did for you on the cross.)

Thought: Now that I am part of the family of God and have a new life, what will I do for the Lord with my past? Have I learned that with God all things are possible?

Reflection:

Part III

Fortress of Security: Walking in Freedom

One by One

As I stand in front of the clinic and the tears roll down my face,
I realize now what happened in this place.
The pain I felt then is nothing compared to now within.
The feelings of urgency seemed so important at the time
that I had to end the pregnancy, and little did I understand
what I was truly doing then.
This little life inside would soon be dying and come to an end.
Emotions were turned off; I was totally numb.
I was frozen from fear and the unknown.

As I look back now, twenty-nine years later,
what was I even thinking?
Yet the truth was nowhere in me, or so I thought.
A still, small voice kept calling for me to stop and turn around,
to lay down my fear and trust by putting my knees on the ground.

I couldn't see the light; at the time I was blind,
guided by emotions and what ifs, forgetting the child I carried inside.
The wall of denial began to grow thick, blocking out the still, small voice.

Not wanting to listen to truth and save this child of mine,
I went about my days as though nothing were different,
trying to act normal around others, all the while hurting deep inside.
I had it all under control; my secret was safe, and my life went on as status quo.
I had everyone fooled, or so I thought
until one day I heard the still, small voice once again.
It was the sound of forgiveness longing to be let in.

This time I listened with tears streaming down my face.
The floodgates opened as I fell to my knees.
I cried like a baby as I came to terms with what I had done.
The Lord immediately showed up, and putting His loving arms around me,
He whispered, "I love you, My child; you are forgiven."

His presence was so thick, I could feel Him at my toes.
Lightness came upon me, and the heaviness I felt arose.
The wall was slowly cracking; His love was penetrating through,
though it would not be till years later the wall of denial
would come crashing down like a ton of bricks,
with Jesus' loving and graceful arms there to catch me.

Digging Deep

They triumphed over him by the blood of the Lamb and by the word of their testimony; they did not love their lives so much as to shrink from death.

—Revelation 12:11

My daughter, I will birth in you a testimony like no other. I will give you a heart after Mine so you can see the hurting heart from My perspective. I will use you to show many women what I can do in their life. I know what you have been through, and I will birth a testimony that will reach deep into the hearts of so many hurting women. Your testimony will be used at times when you least expect it. Be ready in and out of season. There is nothing I cannot do, and your experiences are not in vain. Allow Me to dig deep into your heart of pain and share with others of your healing I gave to you. I wiped the pain away with My blood, and *by the word of your testimony* others will be healed. As the women relate to your pain and the tears begin to flow, there will be a cleansing happening in their heart as it moves into each chamber that needs My healing touch. The tears represent the healing taking place. Tears clear the past and touch deep parts of pain and get in touch with the root cause of hurt.

As healing begins, the cool tears will flow naturally against your cheeks and get warmer as time passes. The deeper your emotions dig, the more healing takes place. It will hurt as you dig deep to the root of your pain. The tears will sting and burn and be hot against your warm, red face. Do not try to control the flow; the more tears flow, the more healing takes place.

Go to the place of unforgiveness that is held captive in your heart. It leads to anger pushed deep inside. Do not cover up the reality with false emotions used as masks to hide the truth. In due time the tears will come unannounced, letting you know there is still healing that needs to take place. As they flow, warm and cool streams seep out of the corners of your eyes, awakening deep hurt buried down in your soul from your past. The tears are reaching the denial you hold deep in your soul. Confront the wall you believed you had given to Me at the cross. You laid it down; now *allow Me to heal you.* It is a process. *As your healing grows, the wall of denial begins to fall down.* Do not be embarrassed and act as if all is well. Be vulnerable, and come to terms with reality once and for all.

The testimony I have for you once you allow Me to heal all areas of your heart will be precious in My sight. I will use your transparency for *My glory* and your personal healing. I love you, My daughter, and nothing is too great for Me to touch with *My healing hands of grace* upon your heart.

 Prayer: Jesus, where did those tears come from? Didn't I give those to You already? Please help me to dig deeper into my buried past and deal with the emotions that are left and allow total healing to take place so I can use this as part of my testimony.

 Thought: What is left inside that I buried long ago with denial?

 Reflection:

Choosing to Walk in Peace

And the peace of God, which transcends all understanding, will guard your hearts and your minds in Christ Jesus.

—Philippians 4:7

My daughter, I am rejoicing over the promise you have made to follow Me and to walk in all the freedoms I have waiting for you. Will your life continue to be worry free, with no more distress heading your way? No, you will have struggles and days of trials and concerns. Worrying about them is your choice. Where there is worry, there is no peace. You now have Me in your life. I will guide you daily as you spend time with Me and allow Me to be a part of your life. I will guard your heart and mind when memories from the past begin to come up. I will help you walk with an *inner peace* as you put your trust in Me. I am in control of your life now. When trials come your way, which they will, My peace will fill your soul and *strengthen your spirit.*

As you choose to walk in My peace I give to you, begin to study the Word of God. Begin to learn the commands I have for you. My Word is filled with lessons to help you get through the difficult times and to help you ask for wisdom when you need it. Be obedient to what I have called you to do. Remember that I am in control as you continue to approach Me with a sincere and transparent heart. My wisdom will flow to your mind, and your heart will be protected from the schemes of the Enemy. The Devil prowls around like a lion, seeking whom he may devour. Stay close to My Word and receive My peace, which will guard your mind and heart against anxiety. I will give you a way of escape when temptation comes and emotional stress lurks at your heart's door once again.

Since you are now in the Family of God, you have taken on the *Mind of Christ.* Feed on the Bible daily and watch your spiritual growth soar with Me. You will mount up with wings as eagles' and soar through the trials of life. I will hold you up during the storms as you choose to walk in peace, trusting your every step with Me.

✝ **Prayer:** Lord, continue to hold my hand as I draw closer to You. Take my life and lead me down a road of peace, claiming victory after victory. When the storms come, I will trust in You, knowing You will make a way of escape for me. Thank you for Your strength as I choose to live as You have called me to.

🐚 **Thought:** When the storms of life come, what will I do to keep close to the Lord and not fall back to an old life?

❦ **Reflection:**

Crossroads

This is what the Lord says: "Stand at the crossroads and look; ask for the ancient paths, ask where the good way is, and walk in it, and you will find rest for your souls. But you said, 'We will not walk in it.' "

—Jeremiah 6:16

There will be times along this journey of healing you will be at a crossroads, having to decide which direction to go. You may go back to your past when discouragement comes your way, or hold firmly to My Word and spend time seeking Me for answers. I will not force you. I am a gentleman and am gentle in Spirit. I want your decision to be that of your own heart. Do not be fully influenced by others that cross your path. Seek My Spirit, ask Me, trust Me; *I will not fail you or forsake you.*

I am doing what needs to be done in your life in order to heal the areas of your life that need healing. Dig deep, My daughter. The more you allow your secret past to be exposed and come out into the open, the more intense your healing. Also, the more freedom you will experience once the chains of bondage to your past come off. The bondage the Enemy had on you is vanished. My one and only Son, Jesus, took it to the cross for you. I loved you so much I sent My Son to die in your place for your sins. He loved you so much He knew He would have to take your place of death and take your sins upon Himself. His act of love gives you a life of eternity with Me in heaven.

My daughter, you will always have a discourager—one against what I am calling you to do, one with unbelief. Do not give in to his or her way of thinking. Be alert to what I have called you to do. *I know the plan I have for you—a plan to prosper you, not harm you; a plan to give you a hope and a future.* People will ridicule you, judge you, and persecute you for My name's sake as they did My Son, Jesus. Do not get disheartened. Stand firm in your decision to follow My Word and be obedient to the calling I have placed on your life. As the temptation comes and the crossroads come at you along your journey, I will fight your battles for you. I will raise up a standard against your Enemy. My child, *I am your deliverer!*

Prayer: As I begin my new journey, Lord, on the road paved for healing, I know I'll come to a place of decision. Please show me a light in the paths I take, so when the Enemy comes in to discourage me and get me off track, I will seek Your face for answers and not get pulled back into what is familiar. Please give me the strength to keep going forward. I will look back only to see how far I've come in my transformation as Your daughter and the healing that has begun to take place in my life.

 Thought: What am I willing to do to take the steps necessary on this new journey of healing?

❧ **Reflection:**

God's Redeeming Grace

For the grace of God that brings salvation has appeared to all men.
—Titus 2:11

My daughter, now that you have accepted My Son into your life, I have adopted you into My family and I am Abba Father. I have been here waiting for you since the beginning of time. I have loved you since before I created you and have planned out your life according to My purpose. *I know the plans I have for you.*

You love My Son, Jesus, because of what He did for you on the cross to transform your life. I loved you so much I sent My one and only Son to take your place and die for you. Now that you have discovered how much I love you, I want you to begin to *crucify your flesh.* This is a part of your nature that the Enemy Satan will tempt you with. Remember, the old man—the person you used to be before you gave your life to Me—is dead. I have opened your eyes and will show you the way to begin walking in My presence with grace, remembering all I have done for you. I will not leave you or forsake you; I will be with you always.

My daughter, I want to take the new you and begin to transform your life radically through your living for Jesus daily. I want you to begin to give Me all your past endeavors that have failed. You have handed over to Me your painful memories of abuse, the pressures of your family, and the hidden sin no one knows about except for Me. Remember, you nailed them to the cross when you accepted My Son. You gave Me your all, didn't you? Allow Me to change your life. *Do not be afraid, for I will be with you.*

I want you to know that it is the *forgiving grace* I give you that enables you to experience My *redeeming love.* Do not go back to your old ways, My child. You have gone from the darkness to the light. I have given you a way to be redeemed by My Son's love. Jesus' blood has covered all your sins and totally forgiven you. Totally let go and receive His forgiveness. There is nothing I cannot cover through His death on the cross for you. *I love you with an everlasting love.*

✝ **Prayer:** Heavenly Father, now that I have given You my life, please help me to totally receive what You did on the cross for me, to accept Your payment for my sins. I don't want to go back to my old ways. Thank you for Your redeeming grace.

🐾 **Thought:** (Take an inventory and see if there is anything left you need to turn completely over to the Lord. Are you holding on to the smallest of sins?)

🌿 **Reflection:**

Your New Master

For such people are not serving our Lord Christ, but their own appetites.
By smooth talk and flattery they deceive the minds of naïve people.

—Romans 16:18

How does it feel, My daughter, to be set free from the condemning voice of your soul's Enemy, which led you to believe you would stay in bondage and never be set free? You so desperately tried to get away from that life, yet the more you tried, the more it seemed fear gripped your heart. You are now free—*free indeed*. You have been delivered by My Son, Jesus, for eternity. No longer do you belong to the world, walking around in confusion, not knowing which way to turn. I have set your feet on My solid ground and turned you from a sinful past to a hopeful future in Me.

You have *a* new Master now. No longer are you a slave to the world. You have found a new dependence on Me and My kingdom. Your mind has been *transformed and renewed*, and you are learning to live a life of righteousness as you pursue the calling I have placed upon you. You will need to stay close to My Word. Keep close to others in your life who share in this same healing as you. Love Me, My daughter, with your whole heart; begin this by obeying My love letter to you. Obtain a Bible and allow My Spirit to speak and guide you. You will not be without sin in your life. The difference is that you will be convicted when you do something wrong and forgiven the moment you confess. Do not let mistakes stay and linger around. They have a tendency to become comfortable, and your feet may slip. Hang on to Me, your anchor for life. *I am your Master who will give you a way of escape.*

Begin to learn who you are in Christ and how you are a part of the Lord's Army. As you follow My Son and He becomes an example for you, trust His guidance as He keeps you on the road to freedom, fighting battles for you. *You know the truth, and the truth will keep you free.*

Prayer: Lord Jehovah, continue to guide me in Your Word. Show me daily, when things get rough, how to keep pursuing You and not give up. My spirit is strong, yet my flesh is weak. Keep me on the right path so I may continue to walk in victory. I know it will not be easy at times, though I know I have You on my side, My Jehovah-Nissi. Thank you, Lord, for becoming my new Master. I am no longer bound to sin, because I have taken up my cross to follow You.

 Thought: Am I willing to spend the time with the Lord in His Holy Word to achieve the blessings He has waiting for me? What am I willing to sacrifice to do so?

❧ **Reflection:**

Who Are You

For we are God's workmanship, created in Christ Jesus to do good works, which God prepared in advance for us to do.

—Ephesians 2:10

You are My princess, the apple of My eye. My plans for you far exceed your own preconceived limitations you have for your life. Yes, you have gone through an abortion with the entire trauma attached, yet I am your Lord and Savior, and I knew that from the start. I had a plan for you, and although your free will took you down an alternate path, I will use your choice for My glory. What the Enemy of your soul meant for evil, I will use for My good. I know all things, and I am many steps ahead of all that goes forth with My creation.

My friend, know you are Mine and you have been bought with a price. The moment you gave your life to Me, My daughter, you were redeemed from **all** your sins. I have adopted you as My child, and I am your Abba Father, the Great I AM. There is nothing you can do to keep Me from loving you. *You are complete in Me.* You can come to Me at any time, seek My face, and cry out to Me. I am never too busy to listen to your plea. It is through My time with you that I can lavish you with My love, dear one.

I chose you at the beginning of time, and you have a divine appointment. I will use your pain for My glory, as I have told you before. You are justified by what Jesus took on the cross for you. When My Son, Jesus, was beaten, it was your punishment He took. His *faithful love* for you led Him to the cross. He was buried. My divine power resurrected Him, making a way for you to become My child and have eternal life. My gift to you is the grace to get you through this life until we meet in heaven one day face-to-face. Your child is waiting, and so am I.

You have been redeemed and called by My name. You are righteous and holy and a blessed saint. You have been set free and made victorious. You are more than a conqueror and joint heir with Christ. *You can do all things through Christ* as you begin your healing journey to everlasting life.

✝ **Prayer**: Thank you, Jesus, for all You took upon Your life to give me the freedom to have a blessed life. You bore my pain and punishment, and You did nothing wrong. You did not deserve The stripes on Your back. Thank you for loving me and the sacrifice You made. Use me for Your glory, and I will continuously give you praise. Allow me to be a light for Your name.

🐝 **Thought:** I can't fathom the pain Jesus bore on my account; what can I sacrifice for Him in return?

✨ **Reflection:**

My Ultimate Purpose

Before I formed you in the womb I knew you, before you were born I set
you apart; I appointed you as a prophet to the nations.

—Jeremiah 1:5

How could you go and make a decision like you did without coming to Me first?
You now know I am the Creator. I created you before you were even a thought
in your mother's mind, and the same is true of your child you lost. I know your
heart ached as the decision was made, yet you did not consider what My heart felt
like. I knew you before time, and I had planned that birth; I had plans for your
child you gave up. Don't be overwhelmed, My child. I knew your decision long
before you even made it, and I saw your heart in the whole process, though I had
hoped a different decision would be made. Because of what I saw and knew was
going to happen, that is why *My loving arms and forgiving grace* are here, waiting
for you to run into them.

Yes, My child, it hurts. The pain runs deep into your soul to such an extent that
you cannot breathe sometimes. Though the choice was made and the procedure
completed, My plans for your life are not new. I will use you for My glory. You
will touch lives, and these women will begin to heal. As I use you as an *instrument
of healing*, you also will continue your healing journey. Go through **all** I need to
take you through. Each step of healing builds upon the next and takes you to new
levels. As the wall becomes bricks alone stacked on top of each other, your healing
will get stronger and run deeper, thus leading to the roots of why you made this
decision to begin with.

You may not see it now, yet when your healing begins and I begin to show you
the reasons why you made this choice, you'll begin to be set free even more than
you are now. My blood brings healing—inner healing, which you need. I came to
earth for you alone. I love you that much. Though your pain is *buried deep inside,*
My love for you reaches just as far.

I will use you, My daughter, to speak to others to help heal their hearts. You
will carry My message of healing and *forgiving grace*, and in return others will
be set free.

✝ **Prayer:** Lord God, speak to me through my spirit and use me to touch other women's lives after my healing takes place. Oh Jesus, use me to be a light to others and see their freedom come to pass. Open up their hearts to be receptive to all you have waiting for each of them. I want to fulfill my purpose for You.

🐞 **Thought:** What am I willing to do, and to what length will I go, to be God's spokesman to those hurting like me, so they can receive the same freedom I've received?

🌹 **Reflection:**

The Father Knows

You discern my going out and my lying down; you are familiar with all my ways.

—Psalm 139:3

My daughter, I love you. I have a purpose and a plan for the sexual trauma I allowed you to go through. I tried to intervene in each situation you were involved in. The times you listened to Me were the times of *obedience.* I blessed you and took care of you. I stopped you from having an unwanted pregnancy. Yes, I know everything about you: your thoughts before you think them, your words before you say them. I know what choices you will make even when I try to stop you from making the wrong one—one that could easily devastate you and cause moral failure in your life. Come to Me with all your burdens, all your sin. There is nothing I do not know. I knew your past, and I know your future—both the mistakes and the achievements.

Because I know your past, I will begin to heal you from that pain caused by all the multiple partners that caused you hurt and left you with an impression of insecurity and abandonment, feeling unworthy and unloved. You gave your heart to these partners, only to find out their intentions were false and meaningless. The men in your life who were supposed to be your protector took advantage of that trust. They made you keep silent and remain in bondage to the abuse and torment they had you in; their cruelty to you was so heartrending you wanted to escape, yet you had nowhere to run to. My child, you need not feel embarrassed to come before Me. Remember, I knew these situations would happen. I know your comings and goings; I even knew when you lay down in the arms of the man you found yourself pregnant with. *"Looking for love in all the wrong places"* is how the world refers to this, I believe.

My ways are not of the world's ways. My ways confound the wise. My thoughts and actions come from a different realm, a realm that will feed you my healing touch and wipe away your sins from existence.

I will tear down every wall of denial and despondency you have built. The memories you have buried alive, I will dig up and bring to pass, into a place of *forgiveness* that only I can provide. This process will not be easy, yet I alone know what you need in order to heal. *My ways are not your ways.* I promise you complete healing at the end of your journey. You have to trust Me. I am your Father in heaven who knows all things and loves you with an everlasting love. I want to see you totally healed and set free of the chains of bondage the Enemy has placed on you. Come and rest in Me and let My loving arms once again rest upon you as you pour out your heart to Me.

✝ **Prayer:** Lord, I want to believe this sexual trauma will be broken and erased from my past. Take thee ugliness I feel and clean it with Your blood. I know there is hope in You and freedom from my past. Shower me with Your love and healing touch. I want to feel worthy and cleansed in Your presence. I want to rest in Your arms of peace, which are waiting for me.

Thought: Am I ready for a new beginning and no longer trapped in the bondage I feel?

Reflection:

Merciful Love

Be merciful, just as your Father is merciful.

—Luke 6:36

I have forgiven you, My daughter, of the sin you committed in your past. I showed you mercy and did not give you the punishment you deserved. In exchange for *My forgiveness and loving grace to you*, you need to do the same for those who took part in your abortion. Give mercy to those who took you to the clinic against your will; show love to the father of the child by forgiving him. Give him to Me, and I will deal with the circumstances. It is not your place to judge or condemn. *All have sinned and fallen short of the glory of God.* No one is perfect, and I will be the judge one day. Until the Day of Judgment, forgive and love the unlovable. Show mercy to them even when it hurts. Clear your heart of all malice and revenge, for revenge is Mine.

Do not judge others, as difficult as that may be. I will give you the strength, and over time you will be able to love once again. Forgive, My daughter, yet you do not have to forget. Forgiving means handing over to me your hurt and grievances that were done to you, allowing me to come into your heart and make it pure before Me. I will give you a *clean and contrite heart.* Your heart that was broken will soon be healed over time.

Come to Me, My daughter, and spend time in My presence. Encounter My love for you as you begin to see the bitterness you've held for so long begin to melt away. Stay close to Me and receive all I have for you. Over time the wounds will be totally healed and you will learn how to forgive those from your past. Give to Me all that surrounds your abortion. Forgive all those involved; feel the mercy I've extended to you. Begin to notice the change in your heart. *Believe.* All things are possible, My child, when you put your trust in Me.

✝ **Prayer:** Jesus, I do need help being merciful to others as you require me to do, especially those associated with my abortion. Show me how to love those who have hurt me so deeply. I cannot even feel the pain anymore because it hurts so much. With your strength I can do this. Thank you for the grace I need and insight which You give to me.

🐞 **Thought:** What will be the gain of being obedient and showing mercy? Do I really want to know the cost of my disobedience?

🌹 **Reflection:**

Victorious Love

No, in all these things we are more than conquerors through him who loved us.

—Romans 8:37

My daughter, it is I, Your Heavenly Father, who loves you with a deep, everlasting love. At times you feel unworthy to receive My blessings because of the choices you have made. Your heart is in deep despair, and you are having trouble getting out of the rut you have allowed the Enemy of your soul to dig for you. No longer do you need to believe his lies. You have been redeemed by My Son's blood and bought with a price. I see you as worthy in My eyes because you have accepted My Son's love and the victory He gave you on the cross.

The shame and deep rejection are no longer a part of your present or future. The guilt and condemnation are not from Me, your Heavenly Father. These feelings are part of the lies you have been fed all this time. Let go, and let Me be in control. Do not be afraid. *I will not leave you.* I accept you as you are, flaws and all. It is through My power and strength that you can carry on. Be brave, My daughter; your *courage* lies in Me. I will give you a sound mind and comfort your spirit; do not be afraid. Give Me your defeat so I can give you your victory, allowing you to walk in freedom until eternity comes.

Permit Me to take you to a place of surrender. If you allow it, I will put you in the palm of My hand to help guide you through your past to a new future in Me. I am a gentleman and will not force Myself upon you. You are a victor, a saint that has won. You have conquered the Enemy through My Son's name because of the love He gave to you on the cross at Calvary. *Walk in freedom* from your shameful past, for I forgive your sins as far as the East is from the West.

✝ **Prayer:** Father, as I spend time with You retracing my past, I thank you in advance for the strength You give me. In You I have a future and a security to walk in freedom in Your Son's name. Through Jesus I am more than a conqueror and I walk in victory. I now know what it is like to experience God's love unconditionally.

🐾 **Thought:** As I give to God my desolation and despair, am I ready to live a life of contentment and courage? What am I willing to do to experience true victory in Jesus?

❧ **Reflection:**

Emotional Healing

The Lord is close to the brokenhearted and saves those who are crushed in spirit.

—Psalm 34:18

I am going to use you, My child. I am here with you, holding your hand in this journey. We will walk together down roads you know not. I am in your life. My Spirit flows through your spirit. My blood flows through your veins, giving you healing power not only physically, but also for the emotional abuse you have experienced, along with wounds left behind. You are not alone. Seek Me; My Word will give you life. Now that your wall has come down and you have dealt with many of your addictions, emotional side effects, and consequences that were behind the wall of denial, and you are on your way to total recovery, I will give you *a pure heart*. Allow Me to show you the way. *Your mourning will now be turned into dancing.* Your love will now flow freely out of you because I flow in you. It is not in your power that you can do all this, but through *My strength* I give to you.

I took your emotional abuse on the cross, just as I did with the sin of your abortion. The emotional abuse you had no control of. In many circumstances you had control over the abortion decision, except those circumstances where abuse and force were implemented. *I came to heal the brokenhearted,* My daughter. You are a part of My family, a large family called the family of God. I will restore your heart, which has been broken. I will put in you the emotions you need to function in a healthy manner. I will give back what the locust, the Enemy of your soul, has stolen from you all these years.

I love you with *an everlasting love.* I made the sacrifice for you and died for all your sins. I took them all when you accepted Me as your Father. I am now *Abba Father, the great I AM*, the Creator. I Am He, your Father. Though your earthly father was not perfect, I will fill your heart with the perfect love you needed to feel and have never received. Know I am with you always and will never leave you or forsake you.

Prayer: Lord, have your presence surround me as I pour out my pain to You. You knocked down my wall of denial. Please help me to pick up the pieces that are new and put me back together emotionally in a healthy way—the way You intended me to be from the beginning of time.

 Thought: What will it feel like to have a new heart filled with the Father's love?

Reflection:

I Am With You

Be strong and courageous. Do not be afraid or terrified because of them, for the Lord your God goes with you; he will never leave you nor forsake you.

—Deuteronomy 31:6

I am your Daddy, that Father you never had. *Fear not, My child*, for it is I that will guide you in life now. I have your destiny in My hands, and *I know the plans I have for you*. Do not worry; worry is not from Me. What you experienced when I set you free is from Me alone.

I have others I put in your life to help set you free. I will use them as time goes on to speak into your life. These women have been down the same path as you and have walked in your shoes like yours in their lives; listen to them. I have sent them to be My mouth with wisdom and My arms to hug you with My love. These women I put in your path feel your pain.

My child, I love you with an *unconditional love*. So do the women I put in your path to comfort you and guide you. Do not be timid. Be transparent with them and share your heart. Cry your tears. These women are My hands extended, and they love you with a love from the Father, which I have given them.

Prayer: Lord, please help me to tear down the walls to my past, allowing me to be open and transparent for those I am going to be vulnerable with.

 Thought: How much of my true self will I reveal?

 **Reflection:**

Hidden in the Closet Part I

So do not be afraid of them, for there is nothing concealed that will not
be disclosed, or hidden that will not be made known.

—Matthew 10:26

My daughter, now that you have become Mine, I am beginning to cleanse your
life of the old things from your past you have hidden deep inside. I will reach far
back into the depths of the corners of your heart, to the hidden places that need to
be cleaned out. Daughter, I will continue to do this cleansing process throughout
your healing journey. I will walk with you, holding your hand and showing you
the way. I will walk with you through the valley of pain and abuse, shame and
remorse. *I will not leave you or forget you.* I have walked this journey once before for
you as I took these experiences to the cross. My body on the cross and the blood
I shed give you the victory already. You now need to walk down the healing road,
go to the battleground, face the Enemy, and claim your victory I have waiting for
you. This is only possible with me by your side.

Open those areas of your life you have forgotten about. I know what is in your
heart. I know the hurt you do not want to surrender to Me. I see your pain that
lingers from the hurt, the abuse you went through, the names that were spoken
over you that hurt like a knife when you hear them today. I feel the rage and see
it in your face when you think about your childhood that was stolen from you.
My child, once again I am here with you. My loving arms wait for you to come
running so they can embrace you with the daddy hug you so need. I want the
tears you have held back for so long to burst out, gushing like a lake through a
broken dam, so you can feel the freedom of cleansing flowing through your soul.
Remember, I forgive you. Receive My love and lasting forgiveness. The agonizing
memories from the past can be placed in My hands. Lay them at My feet and
begin to let them go. Place the painful memories at the cross.

Surrender your will to Me, and allow Me to begin to deal with the issues you
have turned your back on. It is the strength I give you that enables you to face
these situations and deal with these issues and ones of defeat. With Me, there
is only victory! You have to trust me, My child. I am Abba Daddy, the great I
AM. *I am the Heavenly Father, who loves you with an everlasting love. Nothing is
too difficult for Me.*

✝ **Prayer:** Take my hand, Lord, and give me the strength, Jesus, as I go back to my past. Father, give me the courage to face what I see. I thought I had dealt with everything hidden. Please continue to help me clean out the deep issues buried within the caverns of my heart. I now know that with You by my side nothing is too difficult.

🐝 **Thought:** What is stopping me from opening up the door to that hidden issue too painful to face?

🌿 **Reflection:**

Hidden in the Closet Part II

For the Spirit God gave us does not make us timid, but gives us power, love and self-disciplined.

—2 Timothy 1:7

As you take My hand, My child, we will begin to deal with the issue of rejection. It is the bitter root that lies at the depth of your pain. It is at the deepest point. Out of this deep wound of pain pours out bitterness, anger, fear, and resentment. These issues have been increasing for years. The more time that goes by, the deeper they are pushed down and hidden where no one can see the hurt and what is beneath the surface of all your pain. You have covered it up with a mask, living a lie. I want to help you confront each issue.

The root of rejection started long ago, and once we begin to address the hurt and the painful words that were spoken over you, you will begin to feel *My healing touch* in your heart. I tell you now that it will not be easy as you dig through layers, uncovering each one at a time. No longer will the chains that have been holding you captive be there. As you give to me each negative layer of abuse and each negative word spoken over you, you will feel the sting of reality. I will provide you with a way to confront each issue. I will soothe the hurt with My love; My compassion for you is as deep as an ocean. The fears that have invaded your heart, which stem from the painful words spoken over you, will begin to surface. Come to Me with the fears; do not be afraid, *for I did not give you a spirit of fear, but power, love, and a sound mind.* From these fears you have birthed insecurities that sink deeper inside your soul, not wanting to be exposed. Therefore, you put on masks to cover up and hide the truth of what your hurt is actually feeling, allowing no one to get close to you. You do not want to deal with the pain inside your heart, afraid it will only grow until it over takes you. *My yoke is easy,* My child; let Me have the insecurities and begin to show you who you are in Me. *I will make your load light.* I know all. I'm just waiting for you to hand these issues over to Me.

I know you want to be free. You have to trust Me, My daughter; all this will be worth it. You will grow stronger in your spirit, and My presence will *consume you with love* as you share with Me the hidden places of your life. I know what is best for you. Delight yourself in Me, and I will give you the desires of your heart.

Trust Me with the hidden parts in the closets of your heart that have been shut for what seems to be an eternity at times. Commit them into My hands, and I will begin to heal your heart. I know what is best for you. Trust Me. Your Abba Father loves you.

 Prayer: Abba Daddy, please take my fears as I begin to confront each one. I no longer want to feel the pain as I feel it now. I don't even know where to begin. Please guide me and give me a way to heal the hurt. I want to hand each one to You and trust that You will make it all better. Into Your hands I commit my hidden closet and all the pain that lies therein. I trust You, Jesus.

 Thought: Am I willing to face my insecurities and fears head-on to obtain the freedom the Lord has for me?

Reflection:

Secret Is Out

Would not God have discovered it, since he knows the secrets of the heart?
—Psalm 44:21

Here is the secret I was talking about, which is hidden in the closet; you only want a few to find out about it. Now that you are on your journey of healing, My child, others need to be *set free*, and I will use you for *My glory*. Haven't I told you this before? This is no surprise to Me; I ordained it from the beginning of time. I know the plans I have for you, and they will come about in many ways. Do not doubt what I can do. When you gave Me your heart and surrendered your life to Me, I took your desires and began to set them free. You can now walk in liberty. The truth had to be told. Sooner or later I was going to have your secret be known.

Your secret is Mine to do with as I please. You gave it to Me at the cross, don't you remember? It's no longer just yours; it is Mine too, to use to help others heal from the same kind of pain. It will be all right; I'm still on the throne. Some days you will shout it from the mountaintops; other days you will speak words in silence for only Me to hear. Your secret will now be in the open for all to see. Do not be ashamed; walk in the liberty you have gained.

I've healed your guilt; no longer do you hide in shame. The pain is all gone. What is left is the cross and what I did for you, which will now be a part of your testimony; and to Me be the glory! Remember where I have brought you from. *Do not despair.* I love you, My child, and will use all your pain and suffering for My glory. *I am never late; I am always on time.* Trust Me, My daughter, for you do not know what lies ahead, yet I do.

You will always be Mine. Hide yourself under My wings for safety and strength. Come to Me for wisdom and the messages you will share with others. I will speak through you. Allow My words to become your words. I will use you to share your secret with the brokenhearted, whose ears need to hear so pain can be let loose, and whose hearts will be set free; for there is freedom at the cross for others, just as there was for you. My arms were stretched wide open to receive all who come to Me. Hold nothing back, My messenger; your healing is for My glory.

Prayer: Lord, give me the courage to face what is now ahead. My secret is out; now what? What do I do when others approach me? Will I be judged, condemned, or loved and accepted for who You have transformed me to be? Keep me strong in your Spirit, Lord. I can't do this part of the journey alone.

Thought: What's holding me back from surrendering my secret for all who know me to see?

Reflection:

Through God's Strength

I can do all this through him who gives me strength.
—Philippians 4:13

Nothing is impossible, My child, when you put your trust in Me. I will give you the strength you need to go forward and do as I have called you to do. No task is too small; no mountain is too hard for Me to move, for it is I, your Lord, who gives you the *strength* to move through the trials that will come your way. I will be there to help you along the way by giving you wisdom on how to move the obstacles and go forward into heavenly places I have waiting for you.

The things I allow you to go through, My child, will be used for My glory. It is I who will guide you on your path of healing as time goes on. Do not rush things; it is all in My timing, for My purpose and My glory. Your spirit is strong because it is My Spirit that is in you. Do not doubt your strength; *you are a weapon in My hands* to be used to pull down the Enemy's kingdom and set the captives free—*not by your might, but by My Spirit.*

✝ **Prayer:** Lord, You are my strength, my shield, and my sword and buckler. You are my Jehovah-Nissi. You give me the victory over my Enemy. Please remind me who I am in You when the Enemy of my soul begins to try to discourage me from following the call You have placed in my heart. You see and know everything; to you, my El Roi, will I cry.

🐾 **Thought:** When I am weak, what do I need to ask the Lord for and to do in my life to carry me to the next brick of healing?

✿ **Reflection:**

Shining Light

I sought the Lord, and he answered me; he delivered me form all my fears. Those who look to him are radiant; their faces are never covered with shame.

—Psalm 34:4–5

Your journey has begun, My child. There is no more wall to hide behind. I have eliminated it once and for all. I have taken your secret to My grave to give you liberty in Me. No more walls are soaring so high, as if to say, *"My past I totally deny."* The wall you built long ago has begun to crumble, and freedom of your spirit is beginning to shine forth My light. No longer do you need to care about who knows your pain. I have begun to heal you from the pain from your secret. In your past you were fearful of those who might find out, being very careful of how you displayed your emotion around friends and loved ones. Your throat was tight, and your heart ready to crumble; your nerves were on edge, just waiting for the truth to be spoken, and your fear of rejection would be exposed.

Do you still fear from time to time what others would think about you if they knew your secret? All the walls have been knocked down, and there is no purpose to have them exist in your life. You have been healed of your shame. The *chains of bondage* you felt all those years have been unlocked, and you are now free to walk in liberty. You have the Blood of Christ, which covers your sins, and *I remember them no more.* Does the feeling of rejection still linger from time to time, wanting to be a part of your new life, trying to feed your lies of discouragement? Does your mind catch you off guard, realizing the scorn and disgrace you once felt may return, leaving you with a feeling of alienation all over again?

Forget about your past and the haunting questions that try to come your way. You have handed them over to Me, and they no longer belong to you. Continue to fix your eyes on My Son, Jesus, for with Him there is no disgrace. My grace is given to you to give you strength. Your guilt was washed away with My Son's blood. I hear your cry and feel your healing heart. It will take some time, My child; though do not doubt what I can do for you and how I can help you to heal. I have already healed you from all fears and shame. I asked you to trust Me, and I give peace to you. *Your hope is in Me,* and My light will shine on your face for all men to see who you are in Me.

✝ **Prayer:** Father, I know I am healed and covered with Your Son's blood. I no longer need these walls of protection because of all You did for me. Continue to pour out Your grace to me as the Enemy of my soul tries to discourage me from what You have done for me. What's in the past is gone and covered by the blood. Although the enemy tries to shoot poisonous darts filled with fear and shame, it is Your great shield of faith that defends my heart. For it is You in me which is greater than he that is in the world.

🐾 **Thought:** Do I truly care if others find out about my secret? Now that I walk in freedom, what am I going to do with the boldness the Lord has given me?

🌹 **Reflection:**

Accept Your New Beginning

Therefore, if anyone is in Christ, he is a new creation; the old has gone, the new has come!

—2 Corinthians 5:17

Forgiveness is a gift, My daughter, one I gave you long ago. I sent My Son, Jesus, to earth to be born, live, and walk as you do. His life was not easy either, once He became of age. He dealt with the same temptations as you, although the ways He handled them were not the same. The Enemy tempted Him, hoping to get Him to fall, yet Jesus relied on His Father above to give Him the strength that was needed—strength to endure the call He came to fulfill. Jesus' death on the cross was not in vain; it was so you could have *life eternally* with Me. His *death on the cross was His gift of forgiveness* for you; now that you have given your heart to Me, you are free.

Do not punish yourself any longer. Do not hold back; reach out and begin to love yourself, because you have been forgiven. As I have told you before, *there is nothing you can do to forgive yourself of your past.* Jesus did it all when the soldiers nailed Him to the cross. His sacrifice gives you a chance to rebuild and start all over. You have forgiveness, and you are a new creation in Christ as you share with others. There is nothing you need to do to work for your gift or pay Me back. Continue to believe what My Son did for you. Receive His act of love on the cross as a gift, while accepting the blessings I have waiting for you.

The blessings are many for you, My child. Begin to thank Me for them as you praise My name and spend time with Me in prayer, sharing from your heart. I am your friend and want you to know Me. I know you because I formed you.

As you spend time with Me in prayer, this becomes *a weapon for you.* Spiritual weapons, such as praising My name, keeping a steadfast faith in Me, obeying My Word, and continuing to love others and believe in Me, will drive the Enemy of your soul far away from you. *Fight the good fight,* and do not give in. I will be with you daily until you are home with Me in the end.

Prayer: Lord Jesus, as I have been learning who You are and all You did for me on the cross, I have realized that You are my *shield and buckler* and that You fight my battles for me. You are my Jehovah-Jireh. You were the ultimate sacrifice, the sacrificial lamb, that took all my sins. Your gift of forgiveness is free. All you ask for in return is for me to accept and follow You. Please continue to bring me to a deeper knowledge of You so I may be used to help others feel this same freedom.

 Thought: What sacrifice am I willing to make for my Savior to follow Him until eternity?

Reflection:

Blessings from Famines

"The days are coming," declares the Sovereign Lord, "when I will send a famine through the land- not a famine of food or a thirst for water, but a famine of hearing the words of the LORD."

—Amos 8:11

My daughter, now that you are part of the family of God, there is much to share with you. Your trust in Me is the first to work on. I want to liken it to a famine in the land. You are a seed; just as a flower is planted in the ground, so shall I plant you in the midst of rich, dark soil that is full of nutrients even though it is dry and calloused on the surface. As you till the soil to plant the seed, so shall you do the same in your own life. As I recall the memories to you of your past, you will then begin to till the soil, digging emotions up from your past, issue by issue. *You will need to go back to your past to get ahead to the future.* Your healing will take place in this process. Yes, you gave Me your life and I made your heart brand-new. I now want to fill it up with My Word and *loving grace*, teaching you a healthy way to live spiritually, emotionally, and physically. Mentally you will change by taking on the *mind of Christ*. As you read My Word and study its precepts, your spirit man, who is hungry, will grow.

When your life seems to be in the middle of a desert and all is dry around you, offering no comfort at all, begin to look around at My beauty. Find a focal point and hang on, because your victory is right around the corner. I will shine in your life like the sun on a cloudy day, giving you a ray of hope. When the Enemy of your soul, Satan, comes in and tries to discourage you by reminding you of your past failures, remind him of his future flames. That ray of sunshine will light up your spirit to a burning passionate heart of hope for your future. Your past will be turned into passion and will continue to grow, even during the times of famine, until the blessings overtake you.

When you put your trust in Me and believe I will do as I promised, you will have *victory* in your life. Do not give up; keep your eyes on Me, and do not despair. I have a reason for allowing circumstances in your life. As you draw closer to Me, I will move closer to you and *strengthen your spirit*. I have a purpose in all I do. My plan is to *bless you* from the famine.

Prayer: Jesus, as I go back to my past, give me the courage to face what I see. Please help me to find a new hope that comes only from You so You will fill my life with blessings and a future with You. Draw my spirit to Yours. I'm desperate for You, Lord.

 Thought: What are the things the Lord needs me to be thirsty for in my life?

❧ **Reflection:**

Fully Surrendered Broken Heart

"Has not my hand made all these things, and so they came into being?"
declares the Lord. "These are the ones I look on with favor: those who
are humble and contrite in spirit, and who trembles at my word."

—Isaiah 66:2

How transparent you have been before Me, My child. I have seen your heart
and know how much pain you have carried inside for so long. My daughter, I have
heard your bitter and repentant cry; I have felt your sorrowful and regretful ache
inside. I have seen you humble yourself on your knees, pouring out your *broken
and contrite heart.* Your heart *is* pure before Me as you seek My face for answers.
You have boldly come before Me in the throne room and wept uncontrollably. You
have been totally transparent with Me, to the point you are not embarrassed and
ashamed any longer; you are no longer afraid to say what is in your heart and tell
Me all your secrets. You have yielded to Me all aspects of the abuse that you have
encountered over the years. I *listened to the tears* as they dropped in your tear bottle,
sometimes like a flood of water streaming down a waterfall. I have collected each
and every one. Nothing you have prayed has been in vain. Your sincere plea turns
My ears toward your spirit.

Daughter, it is your *broken heart* that draws Me to you. As you humble yourself
and pour out the inner turmoil, I will begin to cleanse you, make you brand-new.
I will work on the inner part of your heart, which not all My hurting children will
allow Me to do. I am taking your anguish and grief and turning it into joy and
relief. Be relieved, My daughter, because you have been *set free* from your secret
and have the freedom to come directly to Me.

Your heart started out closed and calloused at the beginning of your journey; now
you are toward the end of your healing. The heart that was closed up became
broken and contrite before Me. My eyes have never lost sight of your yearning
for healing. Continue to lay your needs before Me in surrender. Wait upon My
timing for your total healing, and trust that I have your heart in My hands. I will
mend it by removing the stone and replacing it with flesh. I promise you, daughter,
there will be *beauty for ashes* and *blessings for your obedience. I am your strength, and
My light shines within you.*

Prayer: Oh Jesus, hear my heart's cry. I no longer want to hang on to anything from my past. I surrender my heart totally to You in faith, knowing it will be totally healed one day soon. I can't carry on any longer in turmoil. This is why I give it all to You. You are my Savior, my everlasting hope, my Redeemer, my Jehovah-Nissi, my Victor! You are Jehovah-Shalom, who brings me inner peace.

Thought: What is left inside my heart that I need to surrender to the Lord? He will give me the grace I need to pull out the turmoil hiding in the crevices of my heart and inner strength.

Reflection:

My Plans for You

"For I know the plans I have for you," declares the Lord, "plans to prosper you and not to harm you, plans to give you hope and a future."
—Jeremiah 29:11

Do you not know, My child, that all I allow you to go through is not in vain? I will use it for My glory. Remember, I am the Creator and have a purpose for everything I allow to happen. What takes place in your life will be used for other women's lives. The situations I want you to experience and take part in may not make sense to you at all. You may wonder, *"Why do I have to suffer like this? What have I done to produce this confusion in my life?"* It is not so much confusion, for confusion is not from Me. When you go through trials in your life, there are lessons to be learned in the midst of them. Yes, there will be pain and suffering once more, and a sense of insecurity. Give Me your insecurities and find the comfort in the midst of your setting.

Be open and transparent with Me, revealing your heart to Me. Now that you have given Me your life and asked Me to be Lord, I have new horizons up ahead for you. *Rays of hope* will come flooding through your life, giving to you a new start. Do not get Me wrong; there will still be days of quietness, days that will not go according to your plan. Remember, I plan your days. Give each one to Me, and allow Me to guide you down the paths I have for you in order to experience the wonder and awe of all I allow you to go through. As time goes on, it will become easier to hand circumstances over to Me, letting Me show you what the next step is. This is going to take trust on your part—a sacrifice you were not accustomed to in your past.

I have your life in My hands. I know the plans I have for you. Your life will be filled with gladness and joy unspeakable. There will be days you won't even be able to contains the overwhelming joy which springs from your heart, because of all I am doing in your life. *"Hold on to your seat,"* as the world says. This is going to be a roller coaster of a ride, one of fun and excitement along with the disappointment and bewilderment. Yet know that I have all things in control just so long as you give Me access to your life. Totally surrender it **all** to Me to posses. Give Me **all** burdens, and take rest in what I am doing in you.

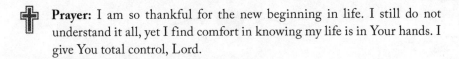
Prayer: I am so thankful for the new beginning in life. I still do not understand it all, yet I find comfort in knowing my life is in Your hands. I give You total control, Lord.

Thought: What do I still need to surrender to the Lord that I have left from my old life?

Reflection:

Heavenly Reunion

But now that he is dead, why should I go on fasting? Can I bring him back again? I will go to him, but he will not return to me.

—2 Samuel 12:23

Now that you have begun to experience the everlasting love I have for you daily and you are learning to walk in My *forgiving grace*, there is still one thing you need to comprehend. Your child is in heaven with Me and waiting ever so expectantly to spend eternity with you. Your child also loves you with an everlasting "mommy love" and can't wait to meet you. I have told your special little one all about you and how much he or she is like you.

At the time of conception, I had all of your child's personality formed. I designed the physical appearance, even down to interests and ambitions. I know all the plans I have for you and your children. I planned each life before time began, and I was waiting to give you your special little one. You will be reunited. Your baby is not an infant, as at the time of development when he or she departed from your womb. Your child continued to grow and has purpose with Me here in heaven. Your child's spirit lives with Me in a new physical form. You see, though the decision was made to end your child's life, I already had plans and a purpose for your child's life if this decision was to be made. I know all things and see all things. Nothing catches Me by surprise.

When King David experienced the loss of his son, he too mourned and grieved. He too had guilt he needed to contend with because of the choices he made. His son's death was a result of his choice to sin. He denied it for a year until it was brought to his attention. When he realized his wrong, he came before Me and wept and asked for mercy. I gave him the grace he needed and gave him *loving mercy*. My daughter, I have done the same for you. Now that you have grieved the loss of your child, given to Me all of your secrets and pain, surrendered all your shame, asked for forgiveness, and received My loving grace, you are ready to meet your child, in due time, face-to-face.

I have given you a new hope and covered your transgressions with My Son's blood. *My healing presence* will continue to be with you, guiding you through life until you come home to live with Me in eternity.

Prayer: Lord Jesus, thank you ever so much for Your hands of mercy on my life. Thank you for what you are sharing with my child, and for taking care of my child's life until I am in heaven at my little one's side. Thank you for Your love, which shines ever so bright on my life, and the comfort You bring to me in the midst of my healing.

Thought: What will be the first thing I do and say when I am reunited with my child one day?

Reflection:

Please Name Me

And the Lord said to Moses, "I will do the very thing you have asked, because I am pleased with you and I know you by name."

—Exodus 33:17

Who am I, do you even know? What would you have called me if I had been able to live with you? I walk around here in heaven, playing with all the others, and like many, we don't know what to call each other. Some of my playmates do have names, and even Jesus calls them by their given name. I asked Jesus one day why I don't have a special name to be called. *"Is it because my mom forgot me and doesn't know what to do?"* I asked. Mommy, I am still a part of you. I look like you in many ways, and Jesus has described you to me. Jesus told me I will see you one day. However, I have to wait patiently.

I miss you Mommy, I really do. I know deep in your heart you miss me too. Do not cover up your hurt any longer. I understand you are doing much better now. You have begun your healing and are on your way to helping others in the same way. You can use our story, Mommy, to help other mommies heal. Do not be afraid of sharing the truth, for God gets the glory.

I forgive you, Mommy; do not be sad. Jesus explained to me what happened. I am not mad. Jesus told me He forgave you long ago, on the cross they nailed His body to; only Jesus knew the victory that one day would be ready for you to have. I know I do not know everything, but what I do know is I will see you one day, along with the rest of my family.

Please name me, Mommy. What is the one special name you long to call me? Jesus knows my name. Ask Him; Jesus will share my name with you. Ask Him my name, and He will tell you in due time. He knows all things and is waiting. He will tell you what I look like and who I am. I want you to be proud of me, Mommy. Please give me a name, memorialize me, and remember me by name.

I love you, Mommy; please do not forget it. Allow Jesus to use you to help other mommies like you so they can see their children one day too.

Love,
Your Child in Heaven

✝ **Prayer:**

🐞 **Thought:** What's my name, Mommy?

🌿 **Reflection:**

Celebrate Your Child

Can a mother forget the baby at her breast and have no compassion on
the child she has borne? ...

—Isaiah 49:15a

My precious daughter, now is the time to celebrate your child. You have gone
back to your painful past to move forward toward your bright future, *walking in
freedom.* You have begun to grieve your loss, so you can now celebrate your child's
life. You have come to Me concerning your child, and I have given you a name
to call your little one. Here are the steps to take to letting go and handing your
child to Me, in order to celebrate life and make your child a part of your everyday
life. I want you to *release your child* to Me. Now that you have begun to heal from
your past, let go and release. *Grieve your loss* in new memories. Name your child
and light a candle, say a prayer, and truly recognize your child for who I created
him or her to be. I will wrap My loving arms around you as you go through this
process of healing. Write your child a letter, read it to him or her, and visualize
your arms holding your little one. Cuddle your precious one and hold him or her
tight, because at the close of the day, your child is in My sight, in My arms to stay
until you greet him or her one day.

Take this time to honor your child; make it a day of remembrance so I may
impart to you total peace for your soul. All is well. Take time to recognize that
this chapter in your life is of utmost importance and will bring closure. It is *a
time of peaceful grieving and heartfelt loss*—one that cannot compare to any other.
The bond you feel with your child is hard to explain, yet with Me you need no
words. For *I see your heart,* which says it all. You are connected to your child, for
I created your child in your womb. Release your child into My arms once and
for all, and mourn the loss. Do not hold back; let the tears flow, for into My tear
bottle they will go.

Celebrate your child's life and cry tears of joy. Your little one is growing in spirit
eternally. I have a purpose for your child's life, and one day soon you will see.
Talk about your child to others, and it will bring healing to your soul, and they
will become even more a part of you.

✝ **Prayer:** Lord Jesus, You are my **Jehovah Shalom,** the one who brings me inner peace concerning my decision that was made. I am truly blessed that You have shown me a way to memorialize my child's death and celebrate life at the same time. The peace I feel can come only from You, for I feel no guilt or condemnation. I feel such a freedom inside that it is hard to describe. I ask You to continue to walk this journey with me and give me the strength to talk to others You put in my path. I want other women to feel the same healing You have given me.

🐚 **Thought:** How do I want to memorialize my child's death so I can begin to celebrate life and keep my child's memory in my mind until I see my little one in heaven?

🌹 **Reflection:**

Celebration Day

But thanks be to God! He gives us the victory through our Lord Jesus
Christ.

—1 Corinthians 15:57

My daughter, I am so proud of you. Look back over your journey with Me and
see how far you have come. You are not the same woman I met with weeks ago.
You can now begin to see yourself as I see you, on your way to total healing.
You have come a long way; it has been a demanding road at times as you labored
with each step you took. The wall you faced in the beginning of this journey is
not the same; these days you have a *new fortress* in Me. The old wall has been
demolished and rebuilt, as was the wall of Nehemiah, My servant of old. As you
faced the old bricks one by one, you surrender each issue to Me and allowed Me
to begin your healing. Beginning to level the wall to the ground was not easy or
pleasant. It took a lot of determination on your part, and you had to surrender
your will to Me. *I gave you the power and strength to face your calloused heart* as
I exposed your issues of the past. I led you to a place of confronting the pain,
digging deep to discover what was behind the mask you wore, while exposing
each chamber of your heart to the reality in which it belonged. My child, you
are a part of My family and have access to the same blessings and inheritance
under heaven all My children do. This is what Jesus came to do, as well as to
forgive you.

You have faced your fears head-on, and in return you have faith to carry on. You
have given me your trust and walk in peace along the road toward an upward
journey to the healing process. You have grieved your loss and handed your child
over to Me. You had to let go, although it was not easy. I gave you closure, letting
you know you would be with your child once again in eternity. They wait for you
as I do. What a day of rejoicing that will be for all.

Your shame is gone, buried forever. Your guilt walked out the door, never to
return, because there is *no condemnation for those in Christ Jesus, My Son.* The
chains of bondage have been unlocked; freedom from sin is what you walk in. I
love you, My daughter, the apple of My eye. There is nothing that can separate
My love for you. All I ask is your obedience to My Word and continued surrender

as time goes by. I will never leave you. Come and hide under the shadow of My wings, and I will protect you.

This is your day to celebrate your freedom. *Love your Heavenly Father.*

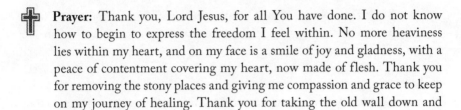

Prayer: Thank you, Lord Jesus, for all You have done. I do not know how to begin to express the freedom I feel within. No more heaviness lies within my heart, and on my face is a smile of joy and gladness, with a peace of contentment covering my heart, now made of flesh. Thank you for removing the stony places and giving me compassion and grace to keep on my journey of healing. Thank you for taking the old wall down and building a fortress in You.

Thought: What will I continue to do to add to the new fortress in the Lord, which now gives me protection from my past?

Reflection:

Share Your Story

They Triumphed over him by the blood of the Lamb and by the word of their testimony; they did not love their lives so much as to shrink form death.

—Revelation 12:11

My daughter, let us stroll down memory lane for a minute. Reflect back to your way of life before I became a part of your decisions and you surrendered control to Me. You were doing your own thing, not even considering the consequences of many of your actions, living life carelessly and not concerning yourself with whose lives were affected by your behavior. Daughter, you were in the world's way. Sin was part of your life, and you were not even aware; maybe you just dabbled and amused yourself in what came your way. My child, when you gave in to the traps of this world, the Enemy of your soul got a foothold and pulled you under until you could no longer breathe, drowning you in a life full of misery. You set your goals and chose your own path to reach them, yet somewhere along your journey, an event prevented you from moving forward.

Your predicament involved a new life, which was not in your plans. Either by force or voluntarily, the decision was made; afterward, your life was not the same. You knew deep down this emptiness could only go on for so long. Finally your eyes were opened and you saw the truth. Down on your knees you went, and you surrendered all to Me. *I have picked you up out of the miry clay, and on solid ground you will now stay.*

My daughter, you need to share your story with others so they too may be healed. It will all be in My timing; depend on Me. I will not fail. I know those you need to touch, including the fathers who need My healing touch. You are not alone in this plight. It will not be easy, and it will not be without a fight. The Enemy of your soul will discourage you. Stay close to My Word and see where I take you.

It was through My Son, Jesus, that I set you free. You accepted Him, and thus you accepted Me. I am Abba Daddy. Share this with others. It is *My healing grace and loving mercy* that sets them free. Share your story, My dear child. Do not hold back. Listen to My voice, and I will guide you. Use your pain for others' gain, and then see the light I shine in you for My glory.

✝ **Prayer:** Oh Jesus, use me as a tool in Your hands, as You are the potter and I am the clay. Show me how to help others heal by the words I say. Use me to see others get free and cross over the Jordan; to help others to claim their victory and walk in healing.

🐌 **Thought:** How transparent am I willing to be when I share my testimony with others? Will I dig deep or stay shallow?

❧ **Reflection:**

Shine for God's Glory

In the same way, let your light shine before others, that they may see your good deeds and glorify your Father in heaven.

—Matthew 5:16

My daughter, now that your healing has begun and you have gained confidence in Me, your Father in heaven, take all you have gained and use it for others who desire the same. I want you to realize that what you hold inside is available to all. Do not try to hide your light behind a wall that does not exist anymore. Do not put on a mask that no longer fits your life. Be that beacon of light others need so desperately. I will guide your every step; I have you covered, and I will not leave you. As you share your testimony, I will shine forth in you a ray of hope to give others. In return, testify of the transformation I have done in your life and praise My name. *Give Me glory and share your story of redemption. I* want others to know they have the same victory waiting for them that they notice in you. Give others hope of their healing, and share all your heart is feeling; it is a heart of flesh to comfort others, no longer a hardened heart of stone.

Many women and men also are walking around in a mask of pain. They too want to throw the mask away, yet they need answers that will come from you as I shine My light in you. This is the time to speak of My goodness and the hope they have in My Son, Jesus. Be the example to others just by how you live your life. Conduct yourself in a holy manner, walking out your salvation daily. I will be by your side with guidance. Remember, no one is perfect, not even you, yet I will give you the grace you need to get through to what I have given you the desire to do.

Shine, My child; shine so bright that others will catch the light you walk in. With Me **all** things are possible; *never doubt.* You have changed and are now walking in your healing. Offer this same healing to others as I go before you preparing the hurt I will put in your path to make you into a beacon of hope. You have been called and given a purpose; others will see your life changed, and I will receive the glory as you walk in victory.

Prayer: Father, continue to shine your light in my life so all I come in contact with will see me shine For You. I am not perfect. I do ask for grace with those You put in my path; please give me the words and strength I need. I praise your name and want You to receive all the glory for all You have done in my life.

Thought: The light that now shines inside of me belongs to Jesus. What can I do to continue to keep this flame for the Lord burning?

Reflection:

Journey Is Not Over

He has shown, O mortal, what is good. And what does the Lord require of you? To act justly and to love mercy and to walk humbly with your God.

—Micah 6:8

The wall has been torn down one brick at a time. No longer do you have to hide, because your pain has been left behind; no longer is it yours to bear. You have given your life to Me, and the future plans I have for you are exciting. My daughter, look back over where you once were and the growth that has taken place within you. You are not the same person. You have been *set free* and are on your way to total healing. As you continue to journey down the healing path, find comfort in knowing I am guiding you daily and you will be used for My glory. The painful past you went through was not in vain; you will be used to help others receive the same freedom.

You have been brought back into right relationship with Me, *restored and redeemed.* In My timing, I will put others in your path, both sisters and brothers in the Lord as well as those who do not know Me as Lord. Share your testimony and be found with favor. Humble yourself and give Me the glory for all I have done in your life. I will give you the words and grace to get through as I have called you to do. *My love and mercy will be extended to you.*

Continue now more than ever to spend time with Me and be sensitive to your call. Continue to obey Me and you will not go astray. The blessing you have on the other side of your healing is that you continue to heal as you serve others. You were saved from your transgressions and past to serve Me, My child, while all along you were healed to bring healing to others. Your healing will continue until we see each other face-to-face. *Your healing is another person's gain.*

When memories resurface, which they will, come to Me and ask Me to search you and take them to the cross. Ask Me what you need to deal with and confront. Healing is an ongoing blessing in disguise. You will be used as a light of freedom in another person's life. Your victory goes from glory to glory as you walk this journey with Me. So hold My hand, daughter, and venture out with Me. Be *bold* and *courageous,* and go where many will not. Testify for Me and give the Enemy a big black eye! He is defeated, and you have received a new life. It will not be boring; you have an exciting future in store. I have instilled in you the passion; now run the race I have set before you.

 Prayer: Lord Jesus, use me; Father, I pray. Let me be used to reach the women who are silent, afraid of their secret being known. Please give them the freedom that You have given me, and use me for Your glory. I know that with Your guidance others will walk in the freedom I have received and their healing will continue daily over time.

 Thought: Lord Jesus, show me what part of my redemptive story adds fuel to the flame in sharing my testimony.

✎ **Reflection:**

Psalm 139

1 O Lord, you have searched me
  and you know me.
2 You know when I sit and when I rise;
  you perceive my thoughts from afar.
3 You discern my going out and my lying down;
  you are familiar with all my ways.
4 Before a word is on my tongue
  you know it completely, O Lord.

5 You hem me in – behind and before;
  you have laid your hand upon me.
6 Such knowledge is too wonderful for me,
  too lofty for me to attain.

7 Where can I go from your Spirit?
    Where can I flee from your presence?
8 If I go up to the heavens, you are there;
  If I make my bed in the depths, you are there.
9 If I rise on the wings of the dawn,
  If I settle on the far side of the sea,
10 even there your hand will guide me,
  your right hand will hold me fast.

11 If I say, "Surely the darkness will hide me
  and the light become night around me,"
12 even the darkness will not be dark to you;
  the night will shine like the day,
  for darkness is as light to you.

13 For you created my inmost being;
  you knit me together in my mother's womb.
14 I praise you because I am fearfully and wonderfully made;
  your works are wonderful,
    I know that full well.

15 My frame was not hidden form you
    when I was made in the secret place.
    When I was woven together in the depths of the earth,
16 your eyes saw my unformed body.
  All the days ordained for me
    were written in your book
    before one of them came to be.

17 How precious to me are your thoughts, O God!
    How vast is the sum of them!
18 Were I to count them,
    they would outnumber the grains of sand.
  When I awake,
    I am still with you.

19 If only you would slay the wicked, O God!
    Away from me, you bloodthirsty men!
20 They speak of you with evil intent;
    Your adversaries misuse your name,
21 Do I not hate those who hate you, O Lord,
    and abhor those who rise up against you?
22 I have nothing but hatred for them;
    I count them my enemies.

23 Search me, O God, and know my heart;
    test me and know my anxious thoughts.
24 See if there is any offensive way in me,
    and lead me in the way everlasting.

Dear daughter of the King,

After completion of this devotional, I looked back and I recognized my own healing journey the Lord was completing in me while I was composing these devotions. As I reread each one, I saw the significance each one portrayed. I realized there is absolutely nothing that is impossible for the Lord Almighty to do in our lives. We need to give Him our heart and allow Him to perform the healing He knows needs to take place. As my pastors have said, "*We are all on our own journey. It is a process.*" It is going to take time. We have to put our trust in *God* and believe He will heal us like He promised; actually, He already has!

The brick wall you had several weeks back is no longer the same wall! There are many holes in it, some bigger than others. Maybe the wall is almost demolished. Whatever the case may be, through your healing, you have begun to build a fortress in the Lord. It is an ongoing blessing in disguise.

My prayer for you is now that you have begun your journey with the Lord, stepped out and received God's forgiveness and what His Son did for you, is that you will continue to walk in your victory that is set before you. Walk in your freedom, and do not allow the Enemy of your soul to inch his way back into your life. Keep hold of your healing and use it to share with others; show them the freedom and forgiveness you have been given. Share with them so they can receive healing for their hearts. All shame and guilt are gone; your heart's been set free, restored and renewed in Christ Jesus.

For further healing, reach out to one of the postabortion recovery programs in your local area. You can contact one of the ones listed on the "Resource" page, and someone will help you find help for further healing. I pray you continue to grow and receive what the Lord has for you. You are His child, and He wants to bless you more than you could possibly ever imagine.

I would like very much to hear about what the Lord has done in your life and your story. My ministry is called Hearts Restored and Renewed. You can reach me at the following:

E-mail: kcovert.heartsrenewed@gmail.com
Facebook fan page look under: Hearts Restored and Renewed
Website link: www.heartsrestoredandrenewed.com

Love and Blessings,
Keven Covert

"I can do all things through Christ who strengthens me" (Philippians 4:13).

∽ Resources ∽

Bible Study Programs for Postabortion Recovery

Forgiven and Set Free by Linda Cochrane, published by Baker Books
Healing a Father's Heart by Linda Cochrane, published by Baker Books

In His Arms by Julie Woodley
Restoring the Heart Ministries
631-689-6686
www.rthm.cc

Surrendering the Secret by Patricia Layton, published by Baker Books
813-931-1804
www.surrenderingthesecret.com

Concepts of Recovery: The Journey, by Millie Lace
870-238-4329
info@conceptsoftruth.org

Ramah International
479-445-6070
www.RamahInternational.org

Retreats and Workshops for Recovery

Rachel's Vineyard
877-467-3463
www.rachelsvineyard.org

A Choice to Heal (workshops)
860-267-6393
www.achoicetoheal.com

Postabortion Counseling and Care

First Care Women's Clinic
561-404-9007
www.first-care.org

Gateway Counseling Center
631-662-5197
www.gatewaycounseling.com

Heartbeat International / Care Net Pregnancy Centers
800-395-4357
www.care-net.org
www.HeartbeatInternational.org
www.optionline.org

Life Impact Network
A Woman's Place Crisis Pregnancy Center
813-931-1804
Lifeimpactnetwork.org

Lumina
1-877-586-4621
lumina@postabortionhelp.org

Piedmont Women's Center
864-244-1434
www.piedmontwomenscenter.org

Project Rachel
1-800-593-2273
www.HopeAfterAbortion.com

Restoring the Heart Ministries
counseling for postabortion care and sexual abuse
631-689-6686
www.rthm.cc

YANA Recovery Center
Jamie Cowhick
754-777-9595
www.yanarecovery.com
yanarecoveryserices@gmail.com
Healing for areas of abortion, sexual abuse, suicide, prostitution/strip club dancers, domestic violence, inner healing in many areas of addiction and recovery.

Help Lines for Pregnancy Decision and Postabortion Care

After Abortion National Helpline, 24/7
866-482-5433
Nationalhelpline.org

Life Skills International
www.lifeskillsintl.org

Suicide intervention/serious self-harm
800-273-8255

Recovery for Men

Healing a Father's Heart by Linda Cochrane, published by Baker Books

Missing Arrows, A Bible Study about Lost Fatherhood, by Warren Williams

www.lifeissues.org/men/missingarrows.pdf

www.menandabortion.info

www.Rachelsvineyard.org/men
877-467-3463

Recommended Reading

Burke, Theresa. *Forbidden Grief: The Unspoken Pain of Abortion.* Springfield, IL: Acorn Books, 2002.

Cooley, Nicole. *Into the Light: Rape, Abortion and the Truth that Set Me Free.* Enumclaw, WA: Pleasant Word, 2008.

Hayford, Jack. *I'll Hold You in Heaven: Healing and Hope for the Parent who Has Lost a Child Through Miscarriage, Stillbirth, Abortion, or Early Infant Death.* Ventura, CA: Regal, 1990.

Layton, Patricia K. *A Surrendered Life: A Thoughtful Approach to Finding Freedom, Healing and Hope after Abortion.* Grand Rapids, MI: Baker Books, 2014.

MacArthur, John. *Safe in the Arms of God: Truth from Heaven about the Death of a Child.* Nashville, TN: Thomas Nelson, 2003.

Reardon, David. *Aborted Women, Silent No More.* Westchester, IL: Crossway Books, 1987.

Reardon, David. *The Jericho Plan: Breaking Down the Walls Which Prevent Post-Abortion Healing.* Springfield, IL: Acorn Books, 1996.

Woodley, Julie. *A Wildflower Grows in Brooklyn: From Striving to Thriving after Sexual Abuse and Other Trauma.* Eugene, OR: Wipf and Stock Publishers, 2013.

~ Bibliography ~

Burke, Theresa. Forbidden Grief: The Unspoken Pain of Abortion. Springfield, IL: Acorn Books, 2002.

Cochrane, Linda. *Forgiven and Set Free: A Post-Abortion Bible Study for Women.* Grand Rapids, MI: Baker Books, 1996.

Lace, Millie. *Concepts of Recovery: The Journey.* Wayne, Arkansas: Concepts of Truth, Inc., 2011.

Layton, Patricia K. *A Surrendered Life: A Thoughtful Approach to Finding Freedom, Healing and Hope after Abortion.* Grand Rapids, MI: Baker Books, 2014.

Self-Ruled Antiochian Orthodox Christian Archdiocese of North America: "Abortion Statistics".2000-2014.